How to Publish Your PhD

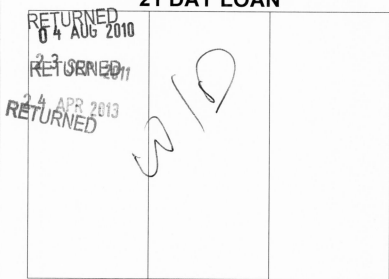

How to Publish Your PhD

How to Publish Your PhD

A Practical Guide for the Humanities and Social Sciences

Sarah Caro

Los Angeles • London • New Delhi • Singapore • Washington DC

First published 2009

SAGE Publications Ltd
1 Oliver's Yard
55 City Road
London EC1Y 1SP

SAGE Publications Inc.
2455 Teller Road
Thousand Oaks, California 91320

SAGE Publications India Pvt Ltd
B 1/I 1 Mohan Cooperative Industrial Area
Mathura Road, Post Bag 7
New Delhi 110 044

SAGE Publications Asia-Pacific Pte Ltd
33 Pekin Street #02–01
Far East Square
Singapore 048763

Library of Congress Control Number: 2008932160

British Library Cataloguing in Publication data

A catalogue record for this book is available from the British Library

ISBN 978-1-4129-0790-3
ISBN 978-1-4129-0791-0 (pbk)

Typeset by C&M Digitals (P) Ltd, Chennai, India
Printed in India by Replika Press Pvt. Ltd
Printed on paper from sustainable resources

CONTENTS

PREFACE

The aim of this book is to provide a basic guide to some of the key questions you will need to address if you are currently undertaking, or have recently completed, a PhD in the humanities or social sciences and are keen to get it published. Whether you choose to follow the advice it contains or not is of course up to you. What really matters is that by reading this book you will be forced to think with some degree of rigor and objectivity about the issues you are likely to come up against when deciding whether to try to get published.

Chapter 1 sets the scene with a brief account of the constantly changing world of academic publishing and some of the key issues currently facing it. Chapter 2 addresses the fact that publication is not always the best option and even if you do decide it is the right one for you, deciding exactly what form to publish in is not always easy. Chapter 3 offers some advice on revising your PhD and adapting the material either into journal articles or into book form. Chapter 4 explores the complexities of navigating your way round the world of academic publishing in search of the right publisher. Chapter 5 focuses on preparing and presenting a book proposal and accompanying covering letter, while Chapter 6 offers some hints on how to survive the review process. Assuming that all goes well Chapter 7 highlights some of the key elements of the average academic book contract. Finally Chapter 8 encourages you to play a pro-active role in the marketing of your book without treading on the toes of your publisher's marketing department.

Indeed the focus throughout this book is on those things you can do to help yourself. It is not rocket science and I suspect there will be no major surprises but it is often the obvious which is overlooked and the small, simple detail that can make the difference between the 'no' pile and the 'maybe' pile.

As I emphasize throughout the book there are no guarantees. Even if you followed every hint, suggestion or word of advice that I or anyone else could offer you, the 'sure thing' of Hollywood films and popular culture sadly only exists in that parallel universe. In the real world of academic publishing it is all about maximizing chances, minimizing risk, a fair dollop of luck and as we shall see in Chapter 1, adapting to a changing environment.

ACKNOWLEDGEMENTS

My first and greatest debt of thanks is to my family – to my parents and sisters for their encouragement and support, and to my husband and children for putting up with me constantly disappearing on holiday, at the weekend, in the evenings, to do a little more work on the book. It has taken me far too long to write this book but without their love and patience it would never have been done.

I would also like to thank the anonymous reviewers for their helpful comments and those of my friends and colleagues first at CUP, and now at OUP, who have taken an interest in the book. Special thanks are due to Martin Green of OUP for his advice on journals publishing. Thank you also to Bryan Turner whose input and encouragement have been as insightful and dryly humorous as ever. I am particularly grateful to all those who answered my plea for help and took time to share their experiences of getting published: Jeff Alexander, Michele Dillon, Kate Flint, Bob Goodin, John Mullan, Keith Oatley, Susan Silbey, Bob Sternberg and Federico Varese. Thanks also to Dr Gita Subrahmanyam at the LSE whose invitation to participate in a seminar on publishing one's thesis provided me with valuable insights and the much needed impetus to finish the book. I owe a very special debt of thanks to Dr Sos Eltis whose kindness in reading an entire draft of the manuscript and providing me with detailed and much needed feedback far exceeded the reasonable bounds of friendship.

Finally my thanks to Chris Rojek for asking me to write the book in the first place and to Chris, Jai Seaman and the rest of the team at Sage for being endlessly patient and supportive through the writing and production process.

Any merit in the book may be thanks to all of these people's input but any faults in it are most definitely mine.

1

THE EVER-CHANGING WORLD OF ACADEMIC PUBLISHING

The aim of this chapter is to provide you with just enough information about the world of academic publishing to find your bearings and with luck navigate your way in due course towards a contract. After a brief overview of the industry as a whole, it then focuses on the key issues preoccupying academic publishers today that are of relevance to the would-be author.

The world of academic publishing is undergoing a significant and prolonged process of change. The days of leisurely lunches and gentlemanly agreements over a glass of port have long since gone. When I first started working as an academic editor it was still possible to pretty much guarantee publication of your thesis in some disciplines as long as you had the support of your supervisor and your supervisor had the right connections. As you will be aware, that is no longer the case. Academic publishing is in many ways like any other billion dollar business. Global markets and the ability to package and repurpose content are key considerations and editors no longer have the freedom to publish what they like. Although the preferences and interests of individual editors can shape a list, ultimately they are simply one more cog in the corporate machine. If the books they commission don't sell they are out of a job, so their commissioning decisions are based not only on the academic excellence of a book but also its marketability and, increasingly, its value as copyright material that can be exploited in a number of different forms. Finding your way around this complex world and making informed decisions is not easy and you will need to have some understanding of this environment if you are to publish your thesis successfully.

One of the key factors you will need to be aware of – and this relates directly to the issue of copyright mentioned above – is the impact of the internet and electronic publishing. The extraordinary advances in knowledge management over the last 25 years have been felt nowhere more keenly than in the field of academic publishing. So completely have these developments altered the mindscape that even those who remember sharing one computer to an office, or hours spent in the university library looking up references with nothing but the books themselves to search through, can scarcely believe such a world actually existed. To use the word 'revolution' in this context for once hardly does justice to the complete change in attitudes and working practices that the advent of the internet and electronic publishing have brought about.

Yet while everyone recognizes the extent of the changes that have occurred there remains little consensus as to their significance. The death of the book has been predicted on numerous occasions with varying degrees of conviction since the 1980s. Clearly reports of its demise were exaggerated and nowadays most predictions about the future of publishing envisage a world where the book is no longer the dominant form but simply one of a number of different formats in which content can be provided.

This multiplicity of formats and publishing models may in some part account for why it is so difficult to predict the future of academic publishing. It may also explain why (in my opinion) there are so few analyses of the business that bear any resemblance to the experience of those who work in it. How do you characterize a business that on the one hand operates like a global industry with a few, huge companies generating billions of dollars worldwide, and on the other includes the equivalent of artisanal studios that produce a handful of carefully crafted books a year and barely make ends meet? Between these two extremes there are of course publishers and content providers of every type and size. Alongside the major scientific, technical and medical (STM) publishers such as Reed Elsevier, Kluwer, Wiley, Springer and Thompsons, co-exist mid-size firms set up by an individual or family (such as LEA or Sage) and a number of American university presses with sizeable endowments which enable them to operate pretty much free of financial constraints. There are learned society publishers, smaller university presses and specialist presses focusing on one subject area such as management studies or social theory. Finally there are others with charitable status like Oxford University Press and Cambridge University Press, who fulfill their charter to pursue the dissemination and furtherance of knowledge at the same time as generating surpluses or profits (in the case of Oxford in significant amounts) which are then ploughed back into the University.

The key issue here is that differences in size inevitably lead to differences in culture. If you work for a large multinational that employs thousands of employees in offices around the world your working practices and attitudes are going to be different to those of someone working for a small university press employing say 30 people all of whom work on the same site. Whether one is better than the other is beside the point and will probably vary from organization to organization. The important thing is to be aware of these differences and their possible implications for you when considering potential publishers. I discuss the various factors you will need to bear in mind when choosing a publisher at length in Chapter 4. For now the main point is that though people often talk about academic publishing as if it were a homogenous field of activity, it is in fact as diverse and multifaceted as most areas of human endeavor and encompasses a huge range of working practices, attitudes, cultures and business models.

Some key issues

Despite these differences, however, there are a range of issues that all academic publishers, be they multinationals or boutique presses, are currently grappling with. Their success in dealing with them will in large part determine not only their own survival but also the nature of academic publishing in the future.

These issues all relate to the revolution in knowledge management mentioned at the beginning of this chapter. The publication and presentation of information and ideas, and the way in which such material is accessed and organized has been totally transformed by the development of electronic publishing and the advent of the internet. Numerous new ways of presenting academic material such as online journals and resource centers, accessed and funded through individual or institutional subscriptions have been developed. You can now buy academic content not simply in book or journal form but in electronic or hard copy, and as much or as little as you want. Amazon for instance offers a service called Amazon Pages whereby you can purchase anything from one page, to a couple of pages, to a whole chapter to view online and Amazon Upgrade allows you to purchase print and online versions of the same text at a specially discounted rate.

Not only has there been a transformation in the way scholarship can be accessed, but also in the sheer volume of material available. Google Print Library has caused some anxiety amongst publishers by announcing its intention to digitalize the full text of all books in the public domain excluded from copyright. Even more controversial was Microsoft's strategic partnership with the British Library to digitize 25 million pages of out of copyright books and then make them available, presumably for a fee, on MSN Book Search and through The British Library National Digital Library. This initiative has now come to an end as abruptly as it started no doubt leaving the British Library much to ponder as it contemplates its future digitization plans.

While many of the world's largest and wealthiest research libraries have for some time been investing millions of dollars in developing virtual libraries of electronic books, these electronic books were created by, and purchased from, publishers. What is different about the Google and Microsoft initiatives is that other kinds of knowledge providers, infinitely larger and more powerful than any publisher, are muscling into their traditional territory and transforming for ever what has been described as the 'information ecosystem.' The fear is that these knowledge providers, unaffected by any native predators, will spread unchecked, so that the existing delicately balanced diversity is destroyed. You could of course argue that this is simply the effect of market forces and a good thing too if it increases customer choice and brings down prices. The danger in the longer term, however, is that if a handful of even the most benevolent organizations control both information and the means to access it worldwide, the end result is a form of, albeit unwitting, censorship. A relatively small group of people would control the definition, creation, development, dissemination and access to knowledge and inevitably the world would be a poorer place, spiritually, creatively and economically. So while one might dismiss some of the concerns expressed as being rooted in self-interest and protectionism on the part of traditional publishers, there are also real issues that all of us need to address.

There can be little doubt then that a major revolution has occurred, one that has had, and will continue to have, wide ranging consequences, not all of them foreseeable. It is also interesting to consider how this revolution differs from that which saw the advent of the printing press 600 years ago. There are clearly many parallels between the issues outlined above and those that faced societies in the fifteenth century regarding the control and use of knowledge. Both revolutions for instance resulted in a greater democratization of learning. The fact that anyone with access to a printing press could swiftly and cheaply produce not only books but also pamphlets, tracts and newspapers meant that there was much greater freedom of expression. New ideas could be circulated widely and quickly, relatively free of the distortions of the scribe or the censorship of the church which until then had a monopoly on the creation and dissemination of scholarly learning. The advent of the internet and the availability of not just books online but also the rich archives of private institutions and elite universities has had an equally liberating effect. For the first time the poor student or scholar living far away from the great centers of learning, possibly on another continent, potentially has equal access to all of the resources of modern scholarship. Previously they may have had to travel great distances or submit themselves to a vetting process, call on referees or sponsors to even be allowed within the doors of the great research libraries. Now they can simply read online those same pamphlets, old newspapers, tracts and historical documents that were made possible by the previous revolution. The pursuit of learning is no longer bounded by the same physical or financial constraints as before, and depends largely on having access to the internet and sufficient intellectual curiosity.

Another common factor is that both print and electronic revolutions have involved technological developments that greatly facilitate the physical manipulation of knowledge. This has enabled readers to search for specific facts and ideas more efficiently and has freed them from the constraints of a linear, narrative development. Consequently both revolutions also lead to the development of a greater variety of forms, in the case of the printing press to the novel and the newspapers, pamphlets and tracts mentioned above; in the case of the digital revolution to the blog, the e-book and the online resource centre. One significant difference, however, is that while the illuminated manuscript for reasons of cost and efficiency was fairly rapidly superseded by the printed book (except possibly as a luxury item), the printed book remains, even in what has been dubbed the digital age, a remarkably versatile and popular piece of technology. It is easy to use, easy to transport, aesthetically pleasing, relatively cheap to produce and requires no other technology to support it. It also has the crucial advantage over the electronic book (at present) that it is much easier to read. Despite the fact that electronic books are able to offer a level of searchability that is very valuable if one is looking for particular references or examples, reading onscreen for long periods of time remains a difficult and unattractive prospect. People dislike reading large amounts of text online so much that they have been known to buy whole electronic books and then laboriously print them up at home in order to read them. They then end up with large sheaves of paper that are neither easily searchable nor manageable.

There can be little doubt that human ingenuity and technology combined will eventually find a way around this problem. Huge amounts of resources have already been invested in trying to develop better reading devices and there was much excitement in the publishing world first over the launch of the Sony Reader, and more recently with the Amazon Kindle. The Kindle is a handheld reading device which mimics the look and feel of a paperback but can store up to 200 books and offers a form of wireless interconnectivity that allows the user to purchase and download additional books at the click of a button. Neither device is cheap though – the Sony Reader was around $299 when first launched, the Kindle $399 – which has clearly limited their mass market appeal. (To what extent is hard to gauge – at the time of writing Amazon were complaining that they could not manufacture quickly enough to satisfy demand). Perhaps the Kindle will be the breakthrough technology but so far no one has developed a device, and in particular a screen, that is as easy on the eye as the printed page. Until they do, any book which depends on narrative flow and the gradual development of complex, inter-connected ideas is likely to remain much easier to read in hard copy than in an electronic version. It is tempting to declare 'The Book is dead. Long live the book!'

Except of course we cannot afford to be complacent. Sales of academic monographs have steadily fallen since the 1970s. Many university presses struggle to maintain their scholarly publishing programmes and it has been claimed that some of them lose as much as $10,000 on each monograph they publish. If this is true in more than a handful of cases it is hard to see how they can survive or indeed how in some disciplines the printed academic monograph can avoid extinction.

Yet it is very hard to be certain whether this contraction in sales is due to the development of the electronic book or to more general market forces. It may be the case in the US, the largest scholarly market in the world, that there are simply too many university presses producing too much product of an insufficiently high standard to satisfy their potential consumers' requirements. What we are seeing could simply be a natural correction in the market. It is hard to tell. Certainly the evidence I have seen seems to suggest that where both electronic and paper copies of the same monograph exist side by side, neither form effects the sales of the other, at least initially. With reference works it seems to be the same though there is some suggestion that over time the availability of the electronic format does erode sales of the paper version. With journals I think there is little doubt that the online journal will supersede the paper version and that the latter will soon, with some few exceptions, be a thing of the past.

The impact of electronic resource centers such as EconPort or the Centre for Hellenic Studies in Washington are harder to judge as they are still at a relatively early stage in their development. EconPort hosts materials for lecturers and students interested in the burgeoning area of experimental economics. It provides a valuable service to that community by acting as a focal point for all those interested in this comparatively new area and brings together materials that would not otherwise be easily accessible. It hosts datasets, some electronic monographs, lab manuals and a textbook. The site for the Centre for Hellenic Studies provides research and teaching materials which have all been carefully vetted by a team of top scholars and includes not only pre-published materials but also an established monograph series, a database on papyri and a journal. It facilitates the review and dissemination of high quality, highly specialized material that might not be commercially viable in printed form. In both these cases it seems likely that rather than replacing traditional printed materials they will continue to provide a valuable service by supplementing and complementing them.

How this affects you

So what do these interesting but rather sweeping developments in the pursuit of scholarship, the preservation of knowledge and the never-ending battle to protect intellectual freedom mean to you? More specifically what is their relevance to getting your PhD published? The answers to this question are manifold but I hope, having read this chapter, reasonably clear.

First of all, when thinking about whether to publish your PhD and if so how, you will need to bear in mind that you are dealing with an industry that is in flux. An industry that faces constant change, and thus faces as many threats as it does opportunities. An industry that is not really an industry and encompasses a huge range of organizations from specialist university presses publishing in only a handful of areas to huge multinationals. As a result you will find a vast range of cultures, working practices and services on offer.

The next most important point is that the advent of the internet and of electronic publishing has caused a revolution not only in the way scholarship is carried out but also in the way it is communicated. Perhaps in part because of the resilience and adaptability, not to mention the user friendliness of the old technology (the printed book), it has hung on side by side with the new much longer than anyone had originally predicted. No one knows how much longer it will last (though my own hope is that it will carry on forever). Whatever does happen there are now a vast range of different ways in which scholarly work can be published and you will need to consider them all carefully before deciding on your preferred option. Some of these different means of dissemination and publication are discussed in the next chapter.

For the record my own prediction is that the printed book will continue to be a significant output in academic publishing in the humanities and social sciences for at least the next 10 to 20 years and that is why much of the rest of this book is devoted to the process of getting your thesis published in printed form. It is also the area in which I have most expertise. Having said that much of what follows will be relevant whatever medium you choose as long as it relies on a process of peer review.

2

BOOKS OR ARTICLES?

A crucial question and it is one you cannot resolve on your own. You will need to take advice from supervisors, mentors and others who have had to make the same decision. You will also need to think about your long term career goals. This chapter will not tell you what to do but will aim to highlight some of the key issues including whether you should focus on journal articles or a monograph or even attempt both.

As you will know from your own experience, people are motivated to undertake doctoral research for a number of different, and sometimes conflicting, reasons. Intellectual curiosity is usually an important factor but not everyone who embarks on a PhD sees it as a stepping stone towards a future career in academia. So the key thing now is to be absolutely, brutally, frank with yourself. Can you really see yourself still working as an academic – hopefully but not necessarily in a tenured position – in 10 years time? Perhaps more to the point does your supervisor think this is a viable option for you? Do you have by now the kind of academic track record that suggests it might be a possibility? If not there is absolutely no point wasting your time and everybody else's in trying to publish all or part of your thesis. It will take a huge amount of effort and much extra writing and editing to fashion your thesis into a publishable book and it will take almost as much work to craft one or two really good articles from it. Such effort, and the inevitable stress that comes with trying to get published, can only be justified if you are seriously planning to commit yourself to a life in academia.

Even if you are hoping to carve a career out for yourself as an academic, publishing your thesis is not always the most productive and career-enhancing use of your time. Given the work required to shape a mass of material that was intended for one purpose into a form that suits an entirely different purpose you may be wiser focusing on a completely new project that is specifically designed to yield results that can be relatively easily transformed into an article or book. The experience of Professor Kate Flint illustrates this point very nicely and also touches on a number of other issues you will need to consider:

I was one of the lucky people who, back in the early 1980s, obtained a permanent job in the UK well before my Oxford D. Phil. (on The English Response to Contemporary Painting, 1878–1910) was completed. By the time it was completed, in 1984–5, it was a loose baggy monster with much information and far too little argument. The most important material in it, on the British response to impressionist painting, had been published as the introduction to a Routledge volume on the Critical Response to Impressionism and I published another chapter as an article in the *Oxford Art Journal*. The dissertation as a whole was a long, long way from being publishable. Happily, I had what I thought was a good idea for what became my first major monograph – *The Woman Reader 1837–1914* (OUP, 1993) – and let the D.Phil. material simmer for a long while, since I knew I hadn't finished with it. Eventually, I returned to some of the ideas and examples in *The Victorians and the Visual Imagination* (CUP, 2000), and two of the chapters, plus a number of stray paragraphs, are based on the old thesis material. The upshot of all of this was that I had a 'real book' out later than I would have done had I tried seriously to publish the doctoral dissertation at the time – but the book was far better as a result than any D.Phil. derived volume would have been at the time.

As Professor Flint acknowledges securing tenure is much more difficult now than it was in the eighties so she was not under the same pressure to publish her thesis as a monograph in order to get a job. Nonetheless she did manage to get two publications from it (even though they were not within her own discipline of English literature) by thinking creatively about the material she had, at the same time as managing to be objective about the thesis as a whole and recognizing that it was not fit for publication as it stood. Undertaking an entirely new piece of research with the intention from the outset of publishing it in book form must have taken some courage but resulted in the book which was to establish her reputation. While returning to some of the ideas from her thesis in her book published in 2000 (15 years after the thesis was finished) meant that she was able to mature and develop her original material into something completely new.

Professor Flint's experience is a testament to her creativity and energy, but what if you don't have a job and are anxious to get one? Is publishing your thesis always the best option?

To publish or not to publish

The reasons for wishing to publish your PhD are fairly obvious. You will have invested several years of your life and a lot of hard work into producing the theoretical analysis or original research upon which your thesis is based. Having made such a strong commitment to a particular project it is hard to let go and it is only natural that you should wish to maximize the potential benefits and advantages that you might derive from it. Why settle for 'simply' securing your doctorate when you could be helping yourself on to the next stage of the career ladder by publishing a book or a couple of good journal articles as well? Indeed in some areas of the humanities such as literature and history there is almost an expectation that you will publish your thesis. If you do not people will wonder why and even assume that you have not sought publication because it was not of a sufficiently high quality. A rather frustrating state of affairs given that a good PhD thesis does not necessarily and indeed, rarely, makes a good book without significant revisions.

The reasons for not trying to publish your PhD are perhaps not so immediately obvious but just as powerful and worthy of careful consideration as illustrated by Professor Flint's example. As we will discuss at length in the next chapter, revising your PhD into a decent book involves a huge amount of work and could well prove as time consuming as writing a new book from scratch. It is definitely not an easy or quick option. Neither is creating a good couple of articles from it. Though it might ostensibly seem the easier option, condensing a whole thesis down into a few thousand words and two or three key points requires significant objectivity, discipline and editorial skills.

There is also the issue of how valuable an addition to your CV it will really be. However hard you work to transform the material into book form it is very difficult to entirely hide its origins and the fact that it is a revised and extended PhD thesis. Unless your thesis was a truly original and outstanding piece of work it will always be seen as just that, your revised PhD thesis, and it will rarely bring you as much credit as an entirely new piece of work. This may seem unfair but is simply the way things are and there is little you can do to change it. It is better to recognize it and plan accordingly, rather than rail against the reality of the situation or try to ignore it.

Having said that, there is always the exception that breaks the rule and makes it so hard to generalize about publishing. This was the experience of Federico Varese, Professor of Criminology at Oxford University:

> I submitted my book proposal shortly after I finished my D.Phil at Oxford. I then worked on the book for some few additional years and the support I got at OUP, especially from my editor Dominic Byatt, was fantastic. The book went on to sell well, got a prize, and has been translated in two languages. At least one more translation is in the pipeline. It also helped me get several jobs!
>
> I would like to make a point: I hear talks from academic publishers against accepting book projects that come out of doctoral work. If it is good for something, my experience proves that books (even those that emerge from PhDs) have to be judged on their own merit.

Two things are worth noting here. Professor Varese's thesis did constitute an original and outstanding piece of work (I know, I was working for a competing publisher at the time and lost it to OUP much to my annoyance!) and he spent 'some additional years' working on it. So the book that was finally published had been considerably developed and revised from the original thesis which formed its core. He also has a point that most academic editors (myself included) are far too ready to dismiss proposals based on PhD theses and that each project should be judged on its own merits. In defense of myself and my fellow editors I would say if only all revised PhD theses were as good as his!

The issue of being dismissed as a regurgitation of your thesis is not quite such a problem with journal articles. By virtue of the fact that they are shorter than a book or thesis and have a clear, readily recognized format, any article that you write based on material in your thesis will, as indicated above, be the product of considerable re-working and editing. If you do a good job of re-writing it and succeed in getting it published it will undoubtedly be a useful addition to your CV as long as it is in a well respected journal. But that is a crucial proviso and we will talk about that in greater detail later.

As well as thinking of the hypothetical benefits that publishing your PhD might or might not bring you, you will also need to think objectively about whether anyone is likely to want to buy or read it. The jury is still out on whether it is better not to publish at all than publish something that fails to meet the highest possible standards but there are other, more tangible tests you can apply to the potential market for your book or article if you decide to try to publish. The most immediate if your work falls towards the harder science end of the social sciences is whether someone has already beaten you to the post and published a similar study to your own. Despite the best efforts of all concerned, this happens more frequently than you would think (at all levels of academic research) and when it does there is little that you can do but shrug and put it down to experience. Of course it is unlikely that another study will exactly replicate your own but there will need to be some significant differences in methodology, results and/or analysis to justify continuing to seek publication.

Similarly, if you are working in a fast moving field such as international trade or intellectual property, it may be that during the time it has taken to complete your doctorate so much has happened in terms of international events or new legislation that your thesis represents an interesting snapshot of a particular period in time but is no longer completely relevant to the current situation.

Finally you need to think about whether the market can simply take another book or article on gender in Shakespeare or the sociology of the body, although the chances are your thesis will have an even narrower focus and be even more difficult to market than either of these well published areas. What makes a good topic for a PhD thesis does not necessarily (one might even go so far as to say, rarely) makes a good topic for a book. Though you should already be familiar with the relevant literature, it would be a useful exercise at this point to go into your local library or campus bookshop (or type a few key words into Amazon) to see just how many books there are already out there on a similar subject. Having identified the five or ten closest matches, try drawing up a list of ways in which your book would be similar or different from them and what your book would offer the reader that none of the other books could provide.

If, having completed this exercise (and found that there is sufficient material that is different and new) and considered all the reasons for not publishing above, you are still convinced that you want to try and publish, the next stage is to talk to your supervisor and other sympathetic academics. Having already spent some time thinking about the pros and cons of trying to publish, and having carried out a little research into the potential market for your thesis, you will be able to engage in a more informed conversation with them. You will for instance, have an idea of the kinds of questions you should be asking such as whether you should go for a book or articles. Or indeed both.

Books

Whether the possibility of turning your thesis into a book is an attractive option will depend in part on your subject area. If you are working in sociology, literature or cultural studies – all largely book-based disciplines – the chances are that it will be. If you work in history, politics and law, you will certainly want to consider the option but will also be interested in the possibility of publishing an article in one of the top journals that dominate your field. If you are a psychologist or economist your sights are likely to be very firmly fixed on journal articles as a route to academic recognition and advancement. To some extent, therefore, whether you decide to go for a book or articles will be a decision that is made for you by the demands of your discipline. But of course things are never quite that easy, especially if you work in an area where books and articles are equally valued. So what other factors might you consider?

The nature of your thesis is obviously one of the most important considerations. Is there sufficient original theoretical or empirical material to sustain a whole book once you have discounted the preliminary material, literature review and methodology? Remember if you go for the book option you may well be looking at a minimum of 60,000 words and you need to have something seriously important and interesting to say to justify that kind of length. Even if you do have lots of important and interesting things to say, do they need lots of contextual material and development to understand them, therefore lending themselves more naturally to book form? Or could they be just as, if not more, effectively conveyed through a series of shorter pieces and articles? The latter is more likely to be the case if you are communicating significant amounts of quantative data and analysis, the former if you have taken a more qualitative or theoretical approach – though this is by no means an infallible rule.

As well as thinking about the material you will be working with, you also need to consider your own skills. Are you a natural writer? Do you enjoy writing? How hard did you find finishing your thesis? If, as many people do, you found the actual writing up of your thesis, as opposed to doing the research, an unmitigated slog and heaved a huge sigh of relief when you handed it over, trying to transform your thesis into a book does not make sense and the shorter, more structured nature of a journal article will suit you better. Conversely if you enjoy writing and have been told by other people that you write well, a book does make sense and could prove a valuable opportunity to develop your skills further.

Another issue that needs to be addressed is how quickly do you need to publish? As we discussed above, if you are working in a fast moving area you will want to get your material out there as soon as possible to avoid someone publishing before you. Seeing a similar study or work published that supersedes your own work before you can get it into the public arena is a dispiriting experience and will render all of the hard work you have put into revising your PhD wasted. If your work is time sensitive it is probably best not to go for a book but to choose articles. I say probably because the time it will take you to prepare at least one good article is likely to be less than the time it will take to produce a whole book, not as you might think because it is always much quicker to publish articles than books. In the strange, topsy turvy world we now live in new technology and the streamlining of the editorial and production process have made printing and publishing academic books much quicker than they once were. The dramatic shake-up of many academic publishing houses' production processes that took place in the 1990s and early 2000s led to much needed cost-cutting, largely through outsourcing of copy editing and typesetting to countries such as India and Singapore. More significantly as far as we are concerned, it led to a significant drop in production times. I was somewhat startled to hear at a recent talk I gave to some postgraduate students that they were under the impression that the average production time for an academic monograph was 1–2 years when in fact it is closer to 9 months.

By way of contrast, the top academic journals, in an attempt to maintain the high standards which are so essential to their reputation and indeed survival, are burdened with a complex and very rigorous reviewing system which struggles to cope with high levels of submissions. There are wide variations between subject areas and between individual journals, so the time from first submission to publication can in some rare cases be as little as 4–5 months but is generally nearer 12–18 months and can be even longer. These significant differences are due in part to varying levels of submissions, but they are also the result of different methods for making submissions. A growing number of journals are now requesting electronic submission which speeds up and simplifies the production process. More importantly, electronic submission is often used in conjunction with open access whereby submissions are posted on the journal's website before, during, and after the refereeing and editorial processes are completed. It is therefore not impossible that your article might be available for all to see within only a few months of submitting it. At the other end of the spectrum if you go with a journal that uses traditional refereeing and production methods and publishes on a quarterly basis, it could easily be a year or two before your article appears in print.

So you should do a little research and find out what the turnaround times are for the journals you are interested in and the average production schedules for the book publishers. This information can usually be found by talking to academics, looking at the journal/publisher's website or by contacting them directly by email. If you contact them directly make your email short and to the point and don't mention any specific article or book as you may get into a premature discussion of the project without getting the information you need. Be prepared for the fact that they will always give you an average time and will refuse to commit to a particular timeframe. This is because production times depend on a number of variables which are not always under the publisher/editor's control such as what state the manuscript is in when it is submitted and how promptly the author responds to copy editing queries. It is also important to note here that what is meant by production time can vary. When I said that most academic publishers can produce a book in 9 months I was referring specifically to the physical process once the manuscript has been finalized of turning it into a book. If the manuscript needs to be read and approved first you will need to allow several more months and it is very hard to say on average how long this part of the process will take. You may find that in some cases, taking into account any final review process and physical production time, that you would get to market significantly faster if you go for a printed book rather than an article, though it may be with a slightly less prestigious publisher. As we will discuss later the rigor of the review process and the speed and quality of the production process vary as much between book publishers as they do between journal publishers and if speed is of the essence you may find it necessary to compromise on one or all of these factors.

The one case where this is no longer true is with publishing online. There are now a number of American university presses who are able to maintain the standards of scholarship associated with more traditional publishing models and combine them with the speed to market usually associated with less fastidious publishers. Once they have put a manuscript through a rigorous review and revision process and it has been approved, they are able to make it available online within a matter of weeks if not immediately if they so wish. It is perhaps slightly surprising that this model has not been more successful or more widely used but like most things it has its plus points and its down sides. While it is fast and generally rigorous, it is difficult to make publishing monographs online work financially and it has still to be widely accepted for some of the reasons discussed earlier. Online publishing of books, unlike journals, is still in its infancy and there remain prejudices about the quality of online material and a reluctance to read large amounts of text online. Where I believe it will really come into its own is with ventures such as Rice University Press which has completely reinvented itself as an online academic press. Not only have the people behind it seen the advantages of editing and producing material electronically and disseminating it through a virtual marketplace and warehouse, but they are also encouraging authors to exploit the full potential of the medium. This means that the scholarly works they produce are freed from the restrictions of paper and ink and can include not only words but unlimited visual material including pictures, computer graphics, video clips and live internet links and audio material of all kinds. The possibilities are endless and very exciting for those engaged in serious scholarship in areas such as the performing arts, art history and cultural studies. Again it remains to be seen how this venture will be judged by the academic community but one can't help wishing them every success.

What kind of book?

A further point to consider when thinking about publishing your PhD as a book is: What kind of book? Should you aim for a multimedia extravaganza, focus on a single author monograph as the majority of people do, or attempt something else?

My own feeling is that unless your thesis started as a multimedia work, to attempt to transform it into one would be overly ambitious at this stage in your career. Such a format is only appropriate in a limited number of subject areas and the editorial skills involved are pretty specialized. While many people now have the necessary technical skills to integrate web links and audio and video clips into a piece of academic research, to do so in such a way as to enhance rather than distract from the argument is more difficult.

There are also issues about the academic assessment and recognition of these new ways of publishing. As discussed above in relation to the online publication of text-based monographs, the technology has been around for a while, but the acceptance of these new media has been slow to come. There still remains a suspicion that the facility with which materials can be published using these technologies means that they can bypass the gatekeeper of traditional academic publishing, the peer review process. While it is certainly true that it is possible to publish unrefereed material directly onto the internet, it is usually obvious that it is just that, and the online publishing and multimedia publishing we have been discussing are all subject to peer review. One of the key challenges going forward for online publishing, however, will be just how rigorous are its review processes? In the case of multimedia publishing for instance, how do you adapt the processes of peer review to the assessment of multimedia presentations as opposed to text based? How do you compare like with unlike? All in all, I think this is an exciting area of academic publishing but also a risky one. If you are thinking seriously about electronic publication you have to be aware that while it might provide you with new opportunities, it also brings the risk that your work may not be considered of equal academic weight to that published in more conventional ways. It is also worth noting that while the majority of established academics when asked will talk about the importance of electronic publishing, when it comes to the publication of their own work, they will seek publication in traditional paper book form nearly every time.

There are no doubt a number of reasons for this, including the difficulty in bringing about a profound shift in academic culture and expectations in less than a generation. The fact remains, however, that the hardcopy, single-authored monograph does offer all the benefits of traditional academic publishing. It provides an excellent showcase for your talents. You are dependent on no-one else either to create your ideas or execute them and the transition from thesis to authored book is the simplest in terms of genre. There are some disadvantages which we will discuss at length in later chapters, not least the real and perceived difficulties in marketing and selling academic monographs in general, and revised PhD theses in particular. But the monograph remains by far the most popular option when considering how to publish one's PhD.

One alternative option which is worth mentioning for the sake of completeness but is only like to be relevant in a very small number of cases is that of turning your PhD into a supplemental text. A supplemental text is a strange hybrid creature, somewhere between a textbook and a monograph and can often be used as a catch-all term for all those books the publisher is not quite sure how to categorize. It is not a textbook because it doesn't just fit one particular course and it is rarely a compulsory student purchase. On the other hand it is not a monograph because it covers a broader subject area and is usually written in a less rarified style. One example of such a text was a book I published while I was at CUP based on a qualitative study of patients with cancer following them through from first diagnosis to their final days. The thesis was written in such an accessible style that once some basic revisions had been made to the chapter on methodology and the literature review, it was a compelling read, of relevance to a wide range of allied health professionals as well as sociologists and anthropologists of health and illness (see further reading). A good supplemental text is difficult to pull off but if you write well and the topic you have chosen for your PhD is sufficiently accessible and potentially relevant to a number of different audiences it may be worth considering.

Finally if you are keen to publish a book and are writing and researching in an area where there are genuinely new and exciting advances being made, it may be worth thinking about putting together an edited collection. There are a number of advantages to this.

First, if you can come up with a good idea for a carefully structured, well-integrated edited book that provides a useful overview of a hot topic, you may well find that there is a real gap in the market and the project is considerably more saleable than yet another monograph. If you can sell the idea to a more senior colleague and persuade them to be the first named editor on the book you will reap numerous additional benefits. You will have your name linked in print with an established academic. You are more likely to be able to attract other academics with a reputation in the field to contribute to your volume, thus raising its quality and profile. You will make many useful contacts for your future career and the chances are that your more senior co-editor will already have publishing contacts which can be exploited to secure a contract. Assuming you are lucky and choose well, you will also have the opportunity to learn much from your co-editor about the combination of diplomacy, patience and ruthlessness needed when giving feedback to colleagues and managing a complex project to a deadline.

Those are the upsides of producing an edited volume but as you will no doubt have already guessed, for every positive there is a negative. Many publishers have a knee-jerk reaction to edited volumes for the very good reason that they have too often had their fingers burnt by hastily thrown together conference papers and poorly edited collections, the latter seen by some cynical and unscrupulous academics as a quick and easy way of getting into print without having to go through the rigors of the journal review process. Unless it is on a hot topic, well structured, and includes a number of top names as contributors or editors, edited collections are perceived as difficult to sell, time intensive and unattractive by most academic publishers. As an editor you are also dependent on the vagaries of your co-editor and fellow contributors. Whatever the delivery date in their contract, there will always be some who are late or even fail to deliver at all so this is definitely not a viable option if your material is time sensitive and you need to publish quickly. Finally, while many co-editors are extremely conscientious, you may be unlucky and find that yours is massively over-committed and doesn't have the time or inclination to put much effort into the project. They may feel that by giving their name and tacit endorsement to the project they have fulfilled their side of the bargain and that it is perfectly legitimate to expect you, their junior colleague, to do all of the hard graft. All in all an edited book is an option you should only consider with caution.

Journal articles

There are a number of reasons why you might decide to try to turn your thesis into a couple of good journal articles. Some of them are the flip side of the coin to why you might choose to write a book as outlined above. Your thesis might be in an area where journal articles count for much and books for very little. It might contain a lot of quantative data and less discursive analysis. The material may be fairly free standing without needing much contextual apparatus. It may be time sensitive (though as suggested above this is a far from straightforward issue). You may not be an enthusiastic writer.

There are also other factors you will need to consider. The number of journals in all subject areas has increased dramatically over the last 20 years. Though there are concerns in the humanities and social sciences as to whether the market can actually sustain so many, in the sciences they are big business and the crucial point as far as you are concerned is that they all need content. Preferably top quality, peer-reviewed content, but they all need content. So in theory and indeed in practice, it should be relatively easy to get your article published. The key question here is *where* you get your article published. Getting published in a low quality journal that has no real status in the field might do your career more harm than good so it is important to identify the top tier of journals in your area and focus your efforts initially on them. It is relatively easy to identify these journals – if you are not already familiar with them – by researching on the internet, checking citations indices and talking to your senior colleagues. In some subject areas (such as economics) academics seem to like nothing better than ranking journals according to various criteria and by typing 'top' or 'best journals' in your subject area into a search engine you can quickly find a number of official and not so official rankings. In less hierarchical subjects it may be more difficult.

A word of caution though. You need to distinguish between the more general subject journals (such as the *American Economic Review* or *Nature*) in which it is incredibly difficult to get published even if you are a well-established academic with a good publication record, and those which are focused on a particular area of the discipline. These latter journals are also difficult to get published in as a first timer but are not impossible and are just as valuable on your CV even if they don't have quite as high a ranking in terms of citations. In other words you should aim high but also be realistic. There is no point submitting to a journal that even your head of department might struggle to get published in. Having said that you should remember that many articles are initially rejected by one journal and then accepted by another. The main reason most articles are turned down is not that they are inherently worthless, or even not quite good enough, but simply that they don't fit the style, interests or focus of that particular journal. Unless you are explicitly told that your article is being rejected on grounds of quality you should immediately try the next journal on your list (bearing in mind that most journals will not consider an article which has been submitted to more than one journal at a time).

You should also be aware that it is quite common for articles to be rejected initially but for the author to be asked to re-submit on condition that they make certain revisions, otherwise known as a 'revise and re-submit'. Exactly what this means varies from journal to journal. In some cases it is tantamount to a conditional acceptance. With other journals there is no guarantee that you won't do all the extra work involved in making the requested revisions only to be rejected again. Unfortunately there is not much you can do in such a situation but quietly accept your lot. If you try to challenge the reviewers'/editors' decision you are unlikely to change their minds but you will make yourself a lot of influential enemies at a time when you need to be making friends. There are a number of excellent books which will guide you through this process, some of which are included in the further reading section at the end of this book. The important point here is that you should not be disheartened if you are not successful straight away. At a recent session I attended on publishing one's PhD, a professor who is now the editor of one of the leading journals in her field, recounted with some feeling her own experiences of trying to publish an article based on her thesis. She was rejected by the first journal she submitted to and was so disheartened that she never tried to get it published again even though she now believes it contained some of the most original work she has ever done. She strongly urged the students there not to give up if at first they met with rejection and very much regretted that there had been no one to give her similar advice when she was starting her own academic career.

Another factor which you should consider when deciding between journal articles and books is dissemination. As we discuss elsewhere, the average academic monograph will, if you are lucky, sell between 500–600 copies in its lifetime. Granted the majority of those sales will be institutional or library sales so with luck more than one person will read them but you will inevitably only reach a limited audience. Admittedly there may not be a very large audience anyway but a big general society journal is likely to have 2–3,000 institutional subscriptions and even the smallest journals are likely to be sold as part of a deal bundled with other small journals to groups of interested institutions, thus ensuring that your article is accessible in electronic and/or paper form to all of the people who are likely to want to read it and some who might not!

Which brings us back to our starting point. Will a couple of journal articles in middle ranking journals help your career more than a high level monograph expected to sell not more than 500 copies? Or to complicate things even further should you try to have your cake and eat it by producing a journal article and a book? Although it is certainly not a good idea to stretch your material too thin, it is quite acceptable to craft one or (in my opinion, a maximum of) two articles from the same original source. As we will see in Chapter 8 such articles can serve a useful dual purpose by adding to your publications list and at the same time raising your profile and advertising a forthcoming book. What is not wise is to slice and dice your material as thinly as someone who once sent me a proposal for a book based on their thesis from which four chapters had already been published as journal articles. In that case there was absolutely no incentive for me as an editor to publish it – quite apart from the hassle of clearing permissions etc, most of the material had already been published and therefore the book could not be seen to make an original contribution to the literature. Nor was their any incentive for anyone to buy the book because the material was already widely available elsewhere. So articles and a book can work but you have to handle it with care to avoid the one undermining the other.

Ultimately the question posed by this chapter – should you go for books or articles or even both – is not one to which it is possible to give a definitive answer. We have explored some of the key issues you will need to consider when making your decision – the nature of your thesis, speed to market, dissemination, your own writing skills – but however scientific and systematic one tries to be there will always be examples that contradict any guidelines or rule of thumb.

Examples like the one I heard recently of a doctoral student who broke all the rules, publishing the results of his doctoral research not in a book, not in an academic journal article, but in one of the most prestigious science journals in the world:

When I was accepted for a PhD in psychology, I had an idea for some research, but it turned out that the department to which I went did not have the facilities for it. So I did something for which they did have the facilities. My experiments came out fairly well, and I wondered what to do about them. Not knowing any better, I wrote them up as a Letter to *Nature*, Britain's foremost science journal. The experiments were only in psychology, not in a proper science like physics or biochemistry, so I was quite surprised when my article was accepted. Then, of course, I took an interest in the journal, and noticed that it published reports of recent research in various fields, so I wrote again to the editors and asked if they would like me to be their Experimental Psychology Correspondent, and look out for interesting studies to report. Again, somewhat to my surprise, they said yes, so I did that for a while. Later, when I started supervising graduate students, the theory I heard circulating among them about how to complete a PhD was: first do the research, then write up, then take a breather, then apply for jobs. I told them that a better theory was to do the research, then publish it, then with some publications it would be easier to get a job, and also there would be less to do when it came to writing the thesis. Without the procrastination of the dreaded writing-up phase, the breather might not even be necessary. After I had got into the idea of writing, it was easier when I came to write my first book. In fact, I rather enjoyed it.

I am sure Professor Keith Oatley, the distinguished cognitive neuro-scientist and author, whose experience this was, would be the first to admit that this was an unusual and unlikely route to publication. In those days a Letter to *Nature* was a short article reporting with a quick publication time, an empirical result and the equivalent today might be rather different, trying to get into a new journal or volunteering a book review for instance. But it does show that one should explore every possibility and while one should always be prepared for the possibility of rejection, as the cliché goes: nothing ventured, nothing gained. He also provides an interesting comment on the value of having one or two of publications on your CV when job hunting and the possible value of writing a journal article as a dry run for writing up the whole thesis. While there are certainly no guarantees that either articles or a book based on your thesis will have a significant impact on your subsequent career, they are unlikely to harm it, and where there are two equally bright candidates for a junior lectureship or research fellowship there can be little doubt that the candidate who has already published or has a contract to publish is likely to be favoured. The one thing that there is absolutely no doubt about is that quality matters, both the quality of the material you finally produce and the medium through which you publish it.

To sum up:

- Do be clear about whether you are committed to a career in academia. It is not worth even considering publishing your thesis if you are not.

- Do try to think objectively about whether anyone else is likely to want to buy or read your thesis. However good it is, it may be too specialized to have a real market.

- Do consider all the different options available to you. Would your thesis be most comfortably reworked into a monograph, published online, or as part of an edited book or one or two good journal articles?

- Do take into account factors such as how time sensitive the material in your thesis is and whether it is primarily theoretical or empirically based.

- Do be aware of the relative status of different journals when considering your options and consult with colleagues and the various league and citation tables available.

- Don't assume that publishing your thesis is necessarily the best thing for your career even if you do decide you want to be an academic.

- Don't opt for journal articles rather than a book simply on the basis of speed to market. There are even greater variations in speed of publication between journals than there are between book publishers and you should check out all of the options before making a decision.

- Don't assume that it is not worth submitting to the more prestigious journals but be realistic.

- Don't be disheartened if you are not successful first time and do keep trying.

- Don't forget quality is all. It is generally worth waiting a few extra months to have an article accepted or a book proposal approved by a more prestigious journal or book publisher than to simply rush into the first opportunity to publish that is offered to you.

3

REVISING YOUR PhD

A PhD performs a specific function, very different from that of a book or a journal. As a result it is structured differently and the tone and approach are not those you would use in a journal or a book. This chapter provides some general advice on revising your thesis and highlights some common problems and issues that will need to be addressed whether you opt for articles or a book, although the focus of this chapter and those that follow will be predominately on book publishing. It includes a practical example of how one might set about restructuring one's thesis into a book and some basic guidelines on content and style.

Unless you are a student of literature the chances are that in your academic career to date you have spent little time thinking about genre or style. You will hopefully have made an effort to write clearly and will have learnt how to lay out references and notes but you may have never consciously considered the genre or format of what you are writing. In fact academic writing like any other form of writing geared to a specific audience is a distinctive genre in its own right and comes with a clear set of expectations on the part of both reader and writer. All academic disciplines conform to the basic strictures of the genre of academic writing, though there may well be significant differences in style which can obscure these similarities.

This point was brought home to me vividly a few months ago when I was attending an interdisciplinary social science conference, listening to a paper by a sociologist while sitting next to an economist. Having spent many years working with sociologists, I thought the presentation was a model of clarity and while it did not arrive at any sensationally new conclusions, made some interesting observations on the way. At the end of the talk the economist turned to me with genuine dismay: 'But he didn't *say* anything'. Allowing for differences of opinion irrespective of disciplinary boundaries, the economist was unable to find anything of interest in the talk he had just heard because it was framed in a different discourse to the one he was accustomed to. Although some numbers were included, there were few graphs, fewer correlations and no discussion of incentives or agents. The economist was not doubting that it was a piece of academic work (though he may have doubted its value) but reacting to the differences in style and discourse between the way sociologists communicate amongst themselves and with others and the way economists do. I should make it clear at this point that I am not suggesting that the only differences between the disciplines of sociology and economics are stylistic. Rather, these stylistic differences emphasize and magnify the existing methodological and theoretical differences which make it difficult for the two disciplines to communicate with each other even when they are studying the same things. This is true of many different areas in which interdisciplinary work is attempted and you will need to be particularly aware of it if your PhD has an inter- or multidisciplinary theoretical or methodological approach. More generally, it is important that you are aware of these differences of style or discourse not only between disciplines but between the various sub genres of academic writing.

Distinguishing between the different types of academic writing

So what are these various sub genres? At the risk of being accused of over-simplifying I would characterize them for the purposes of this book as being five in total: the PhD thesis, the academic journal article, the academic monograph (both electronic and hardcopy), the textbook, and the academic book which crosses over into the general or trade market. In keeping with my previous home-grown definition of a genre as a form of writing that is geared towards a particular audience with a specific set of expectations (whether it be academics or readers of science fiction) I would say that each of these sub genres is designed for a very specific audience and comes with a distinct set of expectations.

A PhD thesis has the unique characteristic of being written for a small and rarified audience that probably knows more about the general subject area than the author – and woe betide any doctoral candidate that forgets it! The author will be putting forward a particular thesis and then trying to prove it at the same time as showing off their knowledge of the related literature and explaining the methodology (empirical, theoretical or both) that they have employed. So essentially it is a defensive document and a showcase at the same time.

The journal article is written by people who know a lot about a highly specialized topic for an audience that also knows a lot about that topic. In a strange way it is not that dissimilar to a thesis in so far as it also has a very specific structure, usually includes sections devoted to literature and methodology, and may well be defensive if the authors are presenting new results or theories. It differs from the thesis in that audience and authors are usually equally well informed so a lot of shared knowledge can be taken for granted. The style is ideally concise and to the point and doesn't allow for self-promoting displays of erudition and verbal wizardry.

The structure of an academic monograph can vary enormously and though it will invariably include references to the relevant literature and explanations of whatever methodology has been adopted it is unlikely to have specific sections or chapters devoted to these topics. Rather they will be integrated into the narrative framework and the emphasis is likely to be less on proving one particular point or presenting one set of results in isolation, but on exploring a range of ideas or results and their implications for a whole area of study. Monographs tend to be written in a fairly technical, academic style but there are plenty of exceptions and those that are written in a more lively style tend to sell better. Even academics hungry for the latest ideas are not indifferent to the way that they are presented and the more accessibly written a monograph is, the more likely it is to find a market amongst graduate students and researchers, as well as other academics. As is the case with journal articles, the author of an academic monograph is able to assume a certain level of knowledge amongst their potential audience but not necessarily the same level of specialization in a particular area.

By virtue of its pedagogic nature the textbook is written with the assumption that the author knows more than the reader. Ideally the style in which it is written should be clear and concise without rhetorical flourishes and its structure will generally be determined by external factors such as the way a particular course is taught, rather than by the internal logic of the material covered. The style and structure of the book will also be affected by commonly used textual features such as chapter outlines, chapter summaries, boxes, definitions, glossaries, further reading, thus making it one of the easiest sub genres to identify.

Finally the academic book which crosses over into the more general market is an increasingly familiar phenomenon, distinguished from other kinds of academic writing by the high advances and celebrity status of successful authors in this sub genre. Yet it is much more difficult to characterize in terms of style, structure or content. There is little similarity between Stephen Hawking's *A Brief History of Time,* Oliver Sachs' *The Man Who Mistook His Wife for a Hat* and Steven Leavitt and Stephen Dubner's *Freakonomics.* They cover different subject matter (astro-physics, clinical psychology and economics), range in readability from the impenetrable to the journalistic, are very differently structured and in all three cases it would have been hard to predict before they were published just how successful they would be. The one thing these remarkable books share in common is the impact they have had not only on their own fields but also on the public imagination.

Identifying similarities and differences: relating style and genre to your thesis

Using the rough guidelines above you can now begin to analyze your own thesis and try to identify those features that are unique to your thesis and those features which are common to the genre. You might even find it is easiest to do this by taking a piece of paper and dividing it into three columns. I will tell you what the third column is for in a minute but for the time being you could put **unique feature** at the top of one column and **feature of the genre** at the top of the next. Feature of the genre should be easiest to start with and might include:

- chapter on methodology
- literature review
- defensive – sets out to prove a specific thesis
- specialist audience
- formalized structure

Unique to your thesis might include:

- original research
- develops new theoretical model
- links a with x for the first time
- applies x method to y problem
- provides first exploration of y over z period of time

Having done that you should then put in column three those features which are common to the sub genre you have decided to adopt and to your thesis. If you are hoping to publish your book as an academic monograph you might have:

- literature review usually integrated into text
- potential audience of academics, researchers and graduate students
- methodology integrated
- tends to explore a range of ideas and results and not focus on a single thesis
- narrative flow and structure important

If you are planning to write a journal article you might put:

- formal structure
- separate sections on methodology and literature
- audience is very specialized
- style is concise

By comparing the three columns you should then be able to identify those characteristics of your thesis which are shared with the genre you plan to adopt and those which need to be changed. You should also have a very clear idea of what is unique to your thesis and needs to be preserved, even accentuated in the final published product.

Down to details: structuring a journal article

Continuing with our examples based on the two most popular sub genres in which people try to publish material from their PhD thesis – the journal article and the academic monograph – let us now think in practical terms about how you might go about restructuring the material you have in your thesis. The most dramatic transformation in terms of length will be for a journal article, but paradoxically it will require the fewest changes to the overall structure. As discussed above the journal article shares with the PhD a similarly formal structure which includes many of the same components. These are an abstract (statement of main thesis), introduction, methodology, results, analysis, conclusions and references. The key difference is length and focus. Ideally you should be concentrating on only one, or possibly two, original studies, experiments or ideas. Though you will be able to establish by use of appropriate references in your introduction and conclusion that you are familiar with the literature you do not want to spend very much of your limited space on this. It will be taken for granted, unless you prove otherwise, that you know the literature and you can take for granted that your audience will know it too. Journals do on occasion publish review articles which focus exclusively on summarizing the recent literature in a particular field. But these articles are always specially commissioned by the journal from people who are already known in the field and may have made a significant contribution themselves. So the important thing is to focus clearly on a limited range of results or ideas and present the most compelling case for the argument you are putting forward. Don't be distracted by peripheral ideas or phenomena, don't digress into long accounts of other work that you have covered in your thesis (you can keep that for another article), stay focused.

Before sitting down to the actual writing up of the article make sure you have read carefully several issues of the journal you are hoping to submit to. Make notes on the style of the journal. How technical is it? Is it aimed at a broad disciplinary audience or a particular specialist group? Is there much data included? Do most of the articles have a continuous narrative flow or are they more summarizing than discursive? Do they have lots of different headings? What is their citation style? And of crucial importance, what is their preferred word length? This last question may not seem to be very important, after all it does not feel as if there is much difference between 8,000 and 10,000 words when you are writing the article, but if you have to edit perhaps 50 articles a year it can make all the difference between whether an article is immediately rejected or considered for review.

Structuring a monograph

Transforming your thesis into a format suitable for publication as an academic monograph may or may not involve much cutting down of length. In fact it may require the inclusion of some additional material or expansion of existing sections (as we shall see below). What is certain, however, is that unless you are exceptionally gifted, lucky, or have been guided by a supervisor who has early-on spotted the publication potential of your work, it will need substantial reworking and restructuring if it is to escape its roots and become a convincing monograph. It is rarely the case nowadays, even in those areas where there used to be series specifically dedicated to publishing theses, to receive a call such as the one Professor Robert Goodin, Distinguished Professor of Philosophy and Political Science received one afternoon:

> I got a phone call from my supervisor's secretary, saying 'Brian was having lunch with the man from Wiley who's overseeing that series of books Brian is editing for them; he says Wiley wants to publish your thesis, so could you please send him a copy!'

And even if you did it is extremely unlikely that it would be published in its original form. As discussed above the average monograph does not follow the thesis–methods–results–analysis paradigm unless it has started life as a PhD and it is usually screamingly obvious when this is the case and the author has not revised it. Recently I received a proposal with the following table of contents (some details have been changed to avoid the person and project being identified):

Chapter 1: Definitions, Empirical Puzzle and choice of case studies
Chapter 2: Literature Review
Chapter 3: Timing, size and composition of X
Chapter 4: Social and political factors affecting X in the Netherlands 1975–1990
Chapter 5: Social and political factors affecting X in Austria 1975–1990
Chapter 6: Some additional factors affecting X in the Netherlands and Austria
Chapter 7: The impact of X in the Netherlands and Austria: a comparative perspective
Chapter 8: Consolidating X in the Netherlands and Austria
References
Appendix 1 a
Appendix 1 b
Appendix 2 a
Appendix 2 b
Appendix 3 a
Appendix 3 b

Of course if I had already completed this book I could have strongly recommended the would-be author read it, focusing on this chapter. As it was I had to turn it down because I simply did not have the time to explain all the changes necessary to turn it into a viable book. It does however, illustrate all too clearly the pitfalls involved in trying to convert your thesis into a book and the fact that however good your thesis is, it does involve a surprising amount of work to make the transition successfully. For the moment we will focus on issues of structure but there were other problems of content and style which I will come back to later.

From our previous discussion of the different features of a thesis and a monograph you will immediately be able to see at least two problems with the structure of the above proposal that might have been avoided. The first is that the author failed to recognize that there is any difference between the structure of a thesis and a book. S/he has reproduced the format of their thesis in its entirety, with scarcely any modification. Secondly and relatedly there is no attempt at narrative flow. The central thesis is announced in the first chapter heading, literature review in the second, the theories and methods are listed in the third and then in rather clunking fashion they are applied to each case in turn (first the Netherlands, then Austria) and finally there is an attempt to draw comparisons between the two case studies, followed by conclusions and a large number of appendices, presumably containing the data upon which the doctoral thesis was based.

In a monograph the expectation is that the constituent elements of a piece of academic work – theory, data, methods, literature – will be integrated into a narrative that frames the book, giving it a distinctive structure and storyline. The reader should finish the book not only having gained some new insight or piece of knowledge but also having arrived there by an entirely new way, even if that route passes through some very familiar territory. In other words, in a book the journey is as important as the destination.

With a thesis that is not necessarily always the case. Supervisors may encourage you to be original in your thinking but the key point of the thesis, as we discussed earlier, is defensive, to state and then prove a particular position. As a result most theses, like the example above, frequent the heavily signposted highways of academic argument. The point is to get as quickly and as efficiently as possible to the essence of what you have to say.

Put in a slightly different way, a good monograph may well include many of the same elements as a thesis but they are presented in a more sophisticated and integrated way. Instead of a table of contents starting with a chapter baldly stating the material to be covered – 'Definitions, Empirical Puzzles and Case Studies' – rather like a list of ingredients at the start of a recipe, the table of contents of a monograph should read more like a menu. It should suggest a series of tempting options to be explored before the end of the meal with each course or chapter synthesizing the elements of theory, data and methods into something new and appetizing, rather than presenting the raw or rehashed ingredients of a thesis.

A monograph may well, therefore, contain what is effectively a literature review but it will be presented in the context of gaining greater understanding of what has gone before or what is to come, not as an end in itself. It may be dispersed throughout the book as different parts of the topic and literature become relevant to the argument, rather than being collected all together in one chapter. Similarly a monograph is less likely to have one chapter devoted entirely to methods, instead methodological issues will be discussed as they arise and except in those cases where methodology is central more detailed aspects will be covered in footnotes or an appendix or even on a companion website.

On the topic of appendices my personal feeling is that it is perfectly acceptable to include them if there is valuable additional material that is too detailed or cumbersome to include in the main body of the text if it helps to illustrate the book's central argument. Six appendices as in this proposal, however, are excessive and as an author you will have to think very carefully about how much of this material is strictly necessary to a greater understanding of the topic under consideration and how much is there simply because it is available. With a thesis it might serve a useful purpose by showing how much data you have amassed but with a monograph less is more and extraneous material may interrupt the flow and obfuscate your argument. Alternatively if you do think it might be useful for the reader to have access to the material, perhaps if they want to follow up a particular theme, you could think about making additional material available on a website, either your own or the publisher's.

Expanding the scope of your book

The final point about structure raised by this proposed outline also relates to content. Chapters 4–8 follow a repetitive structure of looking at x in relation to y, then in relation to z, then in relation to y and z and finally drawing conclusions from all three. To turn it into a viable monograph and appeal beyond a very limited audience (those interested in X in the Netherlands and Austria in a 15 year period) you might want to consider broadening the scope of your study. This may at first seem contradictory advice as I have just said less is more, but by increasing the number of case studies, in this example, perhaps by looking at social and political factors affecting X in a range of European countries, you are substantially increasing the potential market for your book and it immediately begins to feel like a piece of mainstream academic work. While monographs are often by their very nature more specialized than say a textbook or a book for a general audience, they are generally broader in their subject matter than the average thesis. The proposal discussed above shows this clearly and there are plenty of ways in which you can broaden the scope of your book including:

- adopting a comparative approach across countries or times
- applying a variety of methodological approaches to analyzing your data
- including secondary as well as original data
- using a range of theoretical perspectives
- adopting a cross-disciplinary approach
- exploring a particular theme across a whole oeuvre rather than just one particular work/author

Of course this will involve a considerable amount of extra work. It may delay how quickly you can publish your book and you will have to spend some time thinking about how you will choose which additional countries to include in your study (for instance). This decision may be affected by what data on the topic is already available for a specific country, the quality of that data, or how feasible it is for you to collect additional data yourself. You will also need to consider how the new material would be incorporated thus raising new issues of structure and content. In the case of more theoretical work it may involve considerable extra reading around and beyond the areas you have most expertise in to familiarize yourself with new research and debates. Whatever you decide to do, if it looks as if it is likely to involve months of work rather than a couple of weeks do consult with colleagues and advisors and think about putting together a proposal first (covered in Chapter 5) outlining the proposed changes. You can then try it out on a few publishers first and if you get a positive response carry on. If they don't seem very enthusiastic even with the extra material it would be a real shame (not to mention a terrible waste of your time) to put all that work in and *still* not get published. Even if they are enthusiastic as they were in Professor Jeff Alexander's case, it is unlikely nowadays that you would have the luxury of spending five years on further revisions:

I had written a draft of my PhD dissertation by 1974, and was sitting in my small Berkeley apartment reading Weber when the phone rang. 'Hello,' the voice said, 'this is Grant Barnes. I am the Scoiology Editor of University of California Press and just about everybody from Neil Smelser to Seymour Martin Lipset has been telling me what a brilliant dissertation you've written.' 'Really,' I said, my mind spinning. It had never occurred to me that publishing would happen without my trying. I was vastly complimented. But there was more. 'We'd love to publish it,' Grant Barnes said. 'Well, I'd love for you to do it', I said. 'Do you mind if we take a look?' I said, 'Well, it really isn't ready for publication – I'm not even ready to turn it in to my advisors.' 'That's all right', Grant said, 'let us worry about that.'

Three months later, I had a contract. With this in hand, I asked for permission to delay handing it in to write a 'short new introduction' to the 700 page double spaced manuscript. I told the press it would take a couple of months. Five years later, I had thrown the entire dissertation out and written a new one. I had assiduously avoided even speaking to Grant Barnes, much less seeing him, for the previous three years – I was too embarrassed. With the end in sight, finally relieved, I called him. 'Grant,' I said, 'I've got good news and bad news. The good news is the book's done. The bad news is that the manuscript has grown a bit.' 'How much?' he asked. 'Well,' I said, 'it's now about 3,000 pages'. 'I bet it's great,' Grant said. 'I don't know', I admitted. 'Well, send it to us, let us read it, and we'll see.' I did. Two weeks later he called back. 'No problem,' Grant said, 'how would

> you feel about us publishing it in four separate volumes?' 'Pretty great', I replied. That conversation was in 1980. The books came out in 1982–3. My life was changed forever.
>
> I might say that when your work is good, publishing is not a problem. But there aren't many Grant Barnes around any more, are there?

Sadly there aren't, or rather the people are there but the organizations and circumstances have changed so enormously in the last 25 years or so that even the most senior editor would find it difficult to persuade their commissioning board to approve contracting four volumes from a relatively young and unknown academic. But once again it is interesting to note that during the course of those five years Professor Alexander had basically re-written the whole project so that it was essentially new material, even if some of the original ideas had been retained. And I would also agree that if your work is good, you have a very good chance of getting published – though having such supportive and well-known sponsors as Neil Smelser and Seymour Martin Lipset certainly helps!

Putting theory into practice

Before we leave the topic of restructuring completely and turn to other aspects of the revision process, it seems only fair to spend a few more moments on the proposal we have discussed at length as an example of what not to do and consider what the author might have done. The first, most obvious thing is to lose the appendices. One is acceptable, even two on occasion if there is a lot of data or there are important methodological issues, but six is excessive. Second the literature review has to go. That does not mean that all of the material contained in that chapter has to be cut but it needs to be integrated into the text as a whole rather than presented as a self-contained exercise. Next the author needs to think further about the narrative flow of the book. The first chapter should engage the reader and lay out the key themes and substantive areas to be covered as well as the main thesis of the book. It should be an intellectual road map from which the structure of the rest of the rest of the book naturally follows. This may well be what the existing Chapter 1 does but it needs to be presented in a more appetizing way than the current chapter title suggests.

So how might this work in practice? If this exercise is to have any real meaning we need to ascribe a value to X, so let us assume for now, quite arbitrarily, that X stands for immigration, although it could just as easily be the emergence of protest groups, feminist literature, inflation or any one of a vast range of topics. Chapter 1 as we have already discussed needs to map out the structure of the book and its major themes and argument so it needs to have a good catchy title, preferably one that includes the word immigration, the key concept in the book. Chapter 2, currently the literature review, might, in the course of providing some useful background material on previous waves of immigration in Europe, incorporate into this historical perspective a discussion of the way the study of immigration, and in turn the academic literature on immigration, has developed. Note though that in the suggested table of contents below I have limited this to the post-war period. This will be quite a challenge in itself but restricting it to a period of 50 years ensures that sufficient background material is included to provide depth and context but not so much material as to be unmanageable or indeed detract from the main focus of the book. Chapter 3 would then present some empirical data on immigration in Europe, highlighting the methodological challenges involved in collecting such data, and perhaps using the Netherlands and Austria to illustrate this point. Chapters 4 and 5 could be left pretty much as they are but would incorporate Chapter 6 so that they each presented a comprehensive overview of the key factors affecting immigration in the countries they were covering. Chapter 7, now Chapter 6, would focus on the key similarities and differences in the impact and experience of immigration between the two countries. The new Chapter 7 would then build on these findings to discuss the impact of immigration more broadly and to discuss future developments on a European level drawing from the Austrian and Dutch experiences. You would then have a book that looked something like this:

Chapter 1: Exploring the Causes and Consequences of Immigration
Chapter 2: A Brief History of Immigration in Post War Europe
Chapter 3: The Real Story? Issues in the Collection of Immigration Data in Europe

Chapter 4: A Post-colonial Legacy: Immigration in the Netherlands 1975–1990

Chapter 5: Guest-workers and Refugees: Immigration in Austria 1975–1990

Chapter 6: Comparing Experiences of Immigration

Chapter 7: Drawing on the Past, Looking to the Future: Possible Patterns of Immigration in the New Europe

References

Appendix

While the above is a somewhat rough and ready reworking of the material it is intended to give you a sense of the kind of restructuring and the imaginative but practical approach necessary when turning your thesis into a book. Imaginative because you have to step outside the box that has been your thesis, but practical because as we have already discussed there are limits to how much new research you can do and incorporate if you wish to publish relatively swiftly. In this case I have created a sense of a broad canvas through the use of key words in the chapter headings and by providing wide ranging contextual chapters (2 and 7) to frame what are essentially two quite narrow case studies (Chapters 4 and 5). Alternatively you could, as discussed above, expand the time frame to perhaps focus your empirical chapters on immigration in the Netherlands throughout the whole of the post-war period and intersperse some of the material on Austria by way of contrast or comparison. Or vice versa. Or include more countries, but restrict yourself to the shorter time frame. Looking at the outline again I can already see ways in which you might improve it further. You could for instance quite plausibly swap Chapters 1 and 2 around. The important thing is to keep trying things out until you arrive at a new structure you are comfortable with and feel confident that you can flesh out.

Style

How you decide to restructure your thesis will depend in part on the subject matter and discipline within which you are working but there are some more general points regarding style that are relevant whatever your topic and disciplinary background.

One of the most common problems is a too heavy reliance on the opinions of others – in other words too many direct quotes from other critics/theoreticians/scholars. While it is perfectly understandable that you will wish to position your own work in relation to those who have gone before you and show how your own work builds upon theirs, excessive direct quotation can distract from and weaken your own argument and even be quite confusing out of context. It can also become quite tedious if you are constantly referencing the same people and may give the impression that you are less well read than is actually the case (not a desirable outcome!). To avoid this pitfall read through your manuscript looking for opportunities to reduce the amount of direct quotation. Paraphrase or summarize arguments instead of reproducing them verbatim and perhaps cut them out altogether if they are not strictly necessary. Do make sure, however, that you still scrupulously reference any idea that is not your own – the last thing you want is to make yourself vulnerable to accusations of plagiarism.

Almost the antithesis of the kind of intellectual modesty that is constantly referring back to what has gone before is the arrogance of the young and inexperienced writer who feels s/he has nothing to learn from the past or present. This seeming arrogance may be unintentional but whether genuine or not, the appearance of arrogance in a young researcher is very unattractive and will not win you many friends. If you do not wish to appear overly confident be careful how you criticize the work of others. It is perfectly acceptable (and indeed necessary) on occasion to point out the flaws in others arguments or research but the way in which you do so is all important. Dismissing all of the current work in a given field as 'unsophisticated' or 'lacking a strong theoretical underpinning' does not strengthen your own argument but rather suggests that you have failed to understand those of others. To state baldly as was done in another proposal I read recently that 'in my view all these approaches have done their time' is to display a level of over confidence that is not likely to get your own work, however important, treated seriously or objectively. Ironically, the more critical you are of others, the more likely the reader is to be critical of you, so remember: tone is all. Questioning, querying, qualifying are all ok. Ridiculing, dismissing, denigrating are not.

A final general point about style is keep it simple. Good academic writing of any kind is clear, concise and only uses technical terminology where a more commonly used word lacks the necessary nuances or precision.

Although many academics and semioticians would I am sure disagree with me, I personally think that the best academic writing is that which does not draw attention to itself but to its subject matter. There are many fascinating arguments about the symbiotic relationship between words and ideas, style and content, but for the purposes of this book and your first serious piece of academic publishing, you need to concentrate on conveying what you have to say in as direct a way as possible. One of the most frequently heard criticisms of PhD theses is that they are overly rhetorical, attempting to impress by using excessive amounts of jargon and convoluted turns of phrase. If you focus on saying what you have to say as simply as possible your argument will be much more powerful and you will have a much greater chance of persuading the reader of your point of view. The downside of course is that if your argument has any weaknesses these will be apparent straight away. But they are bound to be found out sooner or later and at least this way you have a greater chance of noticing them yourself and addressing them before anyone else does!

Susan Silbey, Head of Department and Professor of Sociology and Anthropology at MIT, has a very interesting story to tell about the importance of learning to communicate ideas effectively and the proactive approach she took to improving her own writing style:

> I completed my dissertation and submitted my first manuscript to the *Law & Society Review*, the most prestigious journal in my subfield of the sociology of law. I was nervous and so excited when the editor replied that he liked the paper very much and would like
>
> *(Continued)*

(Continued)

to include it in a special issue devoted to dispute processing – then a very hot topic. But, he said, although he liked the content of the article, he had serious problems with the writing. He sent me a long review that included a paragraph along the lines of the following: 'I have now received the reviews of your manuscript, and while the reviews are favorable in terms of what the manuscript has to tell us, I simply cannot publish it in the form it is currently written. The writing is rife with problems including such things as inconsistent use of tense, singular/plural problems, lack of parallelism, inappropriate word choice, overwriting, and sentences that fail to convey any clear meaning. You must seek out some assistance and resolve these writing problems before I can put this manuscript into the production process.'

I was shocked and surprised by the letter. My committee had told me that it was a fine dissertation, thorough, imaginative, and original. They recommended it for the dissertation prize of the American Political Science Association. Thus, I didn't see at all what the editor was talking about or what the problems were; the writing looked perfectly fine as far as I could tell and to that point none of my professors had commented on my writing *per se*, only on my data and arguments.

I decided to go to a friend in the English Department at Wellesley College (where I was then an assistant professor in the Sociology Department). The friend took the paper and returned it several days latter with red marks covering the first three or four pages completely. One could see almost no white paper any longer. My friend told me that she could not spend more time on it and told me the old saying about giving a starving person a fish and they have one meal; teach the person to fish and she can eat forever. So, my colleague in the English department offered to teach me how to write. I actually hired her as my writing tutor. Over the next several weeks, I met with my friend repeatedly – for several hours at a time – to work through the issues in the manuscript line by line, learning the meaning of 'active voice,' 'parallel construction,' the appropriate placement of 'only,' the use of 'that' and 'which,' etc. Through this experience, I came to see the nature of the problems the editor was referring to, what I had to do in order to resolve them in the manuscript I was working on, and what I had to be aware of in the writing I did in the future.

I enrolled in a writing seminar with this friend/colleague and became a self-conscious writer of the English language. I memorized Strunk and White and have used it as my bible ever since. (I keep multiple copies in my office and hand them out to graduate students who say that they want to do research with me. Of course, I also give them lessons in research methods and social theory.) Since that first manuscript, I never had an editor comment negatively about my writing, nor have I had difficulty getting published. Eventually, I became the editor of *Law & Society Review* (the journal of that original submission that sent me off to learn how to write), a book series editor (Cambridge University Press Studies in Law and Society), editor of my own collections, and author of my own books.

Having worked with Professor Silbey it is hard to imagine that she ever had any problems with her prose style but this story is a salutary one. It serves as a valuable reminder that even the most gifted and experienced academic writers have to work at their writing and that feedback which can initially seem entirely negative can have very positive results, if acted upon.

Lastly, do not worry if you work within one of those disciplines where many of the most influential figures have very distinctive styles of writing. You will develop your own voice over time as your vision and understanding of your subject deepens. It is not something that you suddenly acquire or can copy from anybody else and it is not something you can force. Study the work of those you admire, concentrate on the mechanics of structuring your argument clearly and saying what you have to say with honesty and simplicity, and in due course your own voice will come.

To sum up:

- **Do be aware of the stylistic and structural differences between the different genres of academic writing.**

- Do identify those features which are original to your thesis and those which are common to the genre so that you can work to enhance the former and minimize the latter.

- Do remember that a journal article needs to be focused, concise and is geared towards a highly specialized audience so you don't need to spell everything out.

- Do bear in mind that in a monograph theory, data and methods should be synthesized and integrated into the text rather than merely described.

- Do be prepared to collect additional material or do extra research in order to broaden the scope and hence the potential audience for your book.

- Don't assume that you simply have to present your thesis as a book for it to be accepted.

- Don't do lots of extra work restructuring and broadening the scope of your thesis unless you are fairly certain that there is interest in it from a publisher and you have a good chance of a contract.

- Don't rely too heavily on the opinions of other critics/academics. Too much direct quotation can be confusing and obscure your own argument.

- Don't write to impress by using lots of jargon and complicated phrasing.

- Don't on the other hand risk sounding arrogant by being dismissive or denigrating the work of others, even if you disagree with it.

4

CHOOSING A PUBLISHER

This chapter offers advice on how to go about looking for the perfect publisher, or at least, if such a thing doesn't exist, one prepared to publish your book. Doing some simple research before approaching your publisher(s) of choice can make the difference between instant rejection or having your proposal sent out for review. Learning to think about books in terms of publishers and imprints, benefiting from other people's experience, prestige vs. speed and accessing the right markets for your book are all covered. The thorny issue of whether you should approach more than one publisher at a time is also discussed.

Unless they are involved in some aspect of the book business, the vast majority of people have no idea or interest in who publishes what book. And why should they? The constant mergers and acquisitions alluded to in Chapter 1 paint a clear picture of an industry which is forever reinventing itself. Bigger companies swallow up smaller ones and then divide and subdivide into endless divisions and imprints. Agents become publishers and vice versa. New publishing and packaging companies seem to be popping up all the time. Not to mention the numerous specialist presses, society presses and university presses, many of them publishing books and journals on behalf of other organizations. The end result is that it is hard for any but the most seasoned industry analyst or those directly involved in the latest restructuring to keep up with the changes.

Perhaps slightly more surprising is the fact that until recently many academics seemed to have had little idea either, even though as a group they have a vested interest in understanding an industry with which, like it or not, they exist in a state of co-dependency. This has begun to change in the last few years as the very multiplicity of options available to them – many of them electronic as also discussed in Chapter 1 – has forced them to think more carefully about their publishing relationships. In the days when the two basic options were print journals or print books whom you were published by only mattered in terms of reputation, the more prestigious the publisher the better. Now it is not simply a question of prestige but of knowing for instance which publisher is publishing actively in your particular field, rather than simply maintaining a presence in it. Are they able to offer an electronic version of your book alongside the hard copy? Might your book be included in an online resource? What kind of sales and marketing resources do they have? An awareness of these kinds of issues as well as some basic understanding of your potential publisher's structure and key markets will help you to find the right publisher. Having found them it will also enable you to tailor your proposal and your approach in such a way that you maximize your chances of at least being taken seriously by them. You don't need to become a publishing expert, but a little homework early on will carry you a long way.

Identifying the key publishers in your area

The first thing you will need to do then is to establish who is publishing actively in your area so you can start putting together a short list of potential publishers. As someone working in academia in the humanities or social sciences, the chances are that you will already have a fair number of books on your shelves either at home or at work. You are also likely to spend a significant proportion of your time reading and looking at books in your subject area either in bookshops or libraries. Take a closer look at the spines and imprint pages. Who publishes those books and under what imprint? It is not enough just to know that a book is published by Taylor and Francis for example (a company that has grown hugely over the last 10 years largely through a relentless acquisitions programme). You also have to know whether it is a Routledge book or Routledge Curzon or Routledge Falmer or Psychology Press. Taylor and Francis books are usually clearly branded but other imprints may not make their allegiances quite so obvious and it is only by getting a good idea of exactly who is publishing what that you have some chance of getting your proposal into the hands of someone who might be interested in it.

Once you start noticing the names of publishers and imprints on the books you regularly handle you may be surprised to find that nearly all the books you use are published by the same small group of publishers. The reason for this is simple. Publishers are essentially conservative creatures. Once they find a formula that works for them they like to repeat it *ad infinitum*. If that sounds like an exaggeration just think of the endless popular psychology books that tried to emulate the success of Oliver Sacks' *The Man Who Mistook His Wife For A Hat* (1985) or the huge number of books on theoretical physics that were published after *In Search of Schroedinger's Cat* by John Gribbin (1984) that were bought by many, read by a few and understood by even fewer. More recently economics and the world financial order have been the flavour of the day and who knows, perhaps in the next few years things might come full circle and books on the environment will be back in fashion again. Aside from the occasional temptation to jump on the latest intellectual bandwagon, however, academic publishers are generally not keen to break into new fields. Indeed the last few years have seen a considerable retrenchment with several leading presses actively withdrawing from, or if they are canny, quietly killing off (otherwise known as a managed decline), their publishing programmes in areas such as anthropology, geography and sociology, areas perceived to be no longer profitable or popular by the big publishers. Whether such judgments are correct and whether they are justifiable is another matter. The fact is publishers are only interested in what works (i.e. what sells) and what fits their current models. This may mean building on a long running series such as *Cambridge Studies in Criminology* or developing a particular niche market such as medieval history or refugee studies. It may also involve rolling out a successful formula such as the high priced, cutting edge professional handbooks by Elsevier North-Holland or the Blackwell Student Companions. Whatever the models favoured by the leading publishers in your area, you need to be aware of who those publishers are and what models they favor so that when you do decide to approach a potential publisher you have a chance of adapting your proposal to suit their needs as well as your own.

Benefiting from the experience of others

Once you have started to think of books in terms of who publishes them rather than simply what's in them, talk to your colleagues, especially the more senior ones who have already published, and ask them about their perceptions of different publishers and their experiences of working with different editors. I am often fascinated when my authors talk about publishing with other editors to hear how differently members of the same industry carry out their business. This is not say that any one way is better than another. Rather as discussed in Chapter 1, there is considerable variation in working practices, expectations and company cultures and it can be useful to have some sense of this when choosing your publisher.

Talking to published colleagues, your supervisor, the people who examined your thesis, could well provide you with some valuable insights into the publishing process from an author's perspective. As indicated above different publishers have very different approaches and while some publishers/editors will expect you to just get on with it once the contract has been signed, others will be prepared to do considerably more hand-holding – figuratively speaking – though this will inevitably depend on how much potential they see your book as having, how busy they are and how nice you are to them!

As the following comment from Michele Dillon, Professor of Sociology at the University of New Hampshire also illustrates, seeking advice from senior colleagues can give you a clearer idea of what to expect and the amount of work involved in publishing your thesis:

I was fortunate to have my first two publications – refereed journal articles – in the same year, 1984. One was based on my master's thesis (on youth subcultures) and the second based on research I was invited to do (on fertility) with a senior colleague. I learned that the publication process runs far more smoothly when you have advice from a seasoned researcher rather than trying to do everything on one's own. Yet, for young scholars, it is not easy to have the courage or self-confidence to ask for advice and suggestions from others. I repeatedly tell my graduate students that writing is hard work and the more drafts one reworks based on comments and suggestions, the better the outcome.

The people you talk to may also have some personal contacts, or at least names, that they are prepared to share with you, the benefits of which are obvious. A recommendation from an established academic that the editor may know by reputation, if not personally, immediately enables them to place your work in some kind of context and will certainly increase the chances of your proposal being considered seriously. A recommendation on its own, however, as we will see in the next chapter is not a guarantee that you will get published.

Publishers' websites

One of the most obvious sources of information about publishers, including what areas they are specializing in, are the publishers themselves. All publishers now have websites where you can access information about their current programme, backlist, organizational structure and instructions on submitting a proposal (more of which in Chapter 5). Although the accuracy and user-friendliness of these websites is not always as good as it should be, spending some time browsing the websites of the key players in your area, and in particular their catalogs will provide you with essential information about their current commissioning programme and will give you an opportunity to think about how your book might fit into it. Alternatively you may also come to the conclusion that your book might not be best placed with a particular publisher because their most recent books are all textbooks and they appear to be moving away from a particular area that they used to be strong in. The important thing to remember is that although (as discussed above) they are essentially conservative by instinct, academic publishers are being forced to constantly adapt. As we saw in Chapter 1 the impact of new technology on the way academic work is produced and disseminated means that if publishers are to survive in what is ultimately a finite market they cannot afford to stand still. As a consequence all publishers – even the subsidized university presses – are regularly analyzing and re-appraising the subject areas and types of books they are publishing. This may mean that although a few years ago a certain publisher had a thriving list in Anglo-Saxon literature or environmental studies, now they may only be honoring their remaining contracts and will no longer welcome new projects in that particular field.

Conferences and Exhibitions

Another very good way to get a sense of which publishers are currently active in your area is to visit the publishers' exhibitions at the conferences you go to. Attending these conferences is a costly and time intensive undertaking and a publisher will only go to the bother of paying to exhibit and staffing it at those conferences devoted to subject areas in which they already have a strong presence or into which they are hoping to move. Half an hour browsing the exhibits and picking up catalogs and fliers is time well spent as you will probably see a greater range of their titles in one place than you are likely to see in any bookshop or library. You will also get a good sense of which titles they are actively promoting. Don't go up to whoever is on the stand and ask them if they would be interested in publishing your PhD as the person on the stand may well be a marketing or sales person who has no direct involvement in the commissioning process. You are also setting yourself up to be politely told no. Do ask them about their key titles for the coming season and which areas they are actively developing. If you establish that they are not an editor ask them to whom proposals should be sent.

Choosing a publisher

Once you have done all of the things suggested above – made a note of who publishes the books you use most often, talked to colleagues, browsed the publishers' displays at conferences and browsed a few publishers' websites – you should be pretty close to putting together a short list of potential publishers. You will know who is publishing actively in your area and whether they are focusing predominately on monographs, reference works or textbooks. You will have a good idea of how well (or not!) they promote their books and you will have acquired a sense of how they are perceived in the academic community. But what other factors apart from reputation (which we will come back to) do you need to consider?

As we saw in Chapter 1 the academic publishing business encompasses every kind of publisher, ranging from huge multinationals to boutique presses. There are large commercial presses, university presses, learned societies and small privately owned presses that only publish a few titles a year. Each of these various kinds of presses will have different publishing models, different audiences and different markets. As a result they will also have very different strengths and weaknesses that you will need to take into account when finalizing your short list. Unfortunately there are far too many academic publishers for us to be able to discuss them all individually but there are some general points worth noting.

Reaching the right markets

By far the most important is the need to find the right marketing fit. Marketing fit is all about making sure that the potential markets for your book match the markets that your chosen publisher can reach.

In the process of revising your thesis for publication as discussed in Chapter 3 you will have already thought about the main markets for your book. These divide into three main components: geographic, disciplinary and end user. For the purposes of academic publishing, geographic market can be divided very roughly into Europe, North America and the Rest of the World (ROW). ROW can clearly be further divided up into a multitude of markets such as Far East, Latin America, Australasia etc., but unless a book is very specifically targeted to one of these areas the chances of substantial sales in them are small, hence the use of generic terms such as ROW or the equally vague 'international markets'. By looking at websites and catalogs you should be able to get a good idea of whether your publisher of choice has branches in parts of the world other than their main office. Sage for instance has branches in California, London, New Delhi and Singapore. Cambridge University Press has branches producing academic books in Cambridge, New York and Australia but also has offices in (amongst other places) South Africa, Singapore and Brazil. Their core focus is on other areas of the business (such as English language teaching materials) but they still act as a valuable centre for targeted promotion of relevant academic books in their territories. Oxford University Press, in addition to offices in Oxford and New York, has active academic publishing programmes originating from its offices in India, Pakistan and South Africa, as well as offices throughout Africa, Europe, Latin America and the Far East. Wiley Blackwell, Taylor and Francis, Elsevier, Palgrave Macmillan (like OUP, CUP and Sage) are also major international companies that you might be thinking of approaching, who have offices in Europe and the US and the resources to effectively market a book with an international market. (There are no doubt many others similarly placed but as mentioned earlier I don't have the room or time to mention every publisher by name.) The advantages of publishing with a company of this size and clout are obvious. As well as being able to market a book to a variety of different markets they have a high level of resources and expertise at their command and established systems for doing so. The disadvantage is that you will be a very small cog in a very large wheel. The systems that ensure you get a certain standard of editing, production and marketing will probably not allow for much deviation from the model and the chances are you won't get a huge amount of personal attention. That is not to say that you won't get any individual care and you may well have an excellent experience but publishing your book with a large company that produces hundreds of books a year will inevitably be a qualitatively different experience from doing so with one which only publishes 50.

Publishing with a smaller, more specialist publisher whose sales and marketing efforts are focused tightly on their core market can be a distinct advantage. Your book may well be given higher profile by a publisher who produces a total of 30–40 new titles a year and you will get the kind of personal care and attention to detail that the bigger presses don't always deliver. The downside is that many of the smaller academic and university presses do not have their own sales forces and are dependent on specialist distributors to reach their markets in Europe and/or the US. This may not be a problem if for instance your thesis is focused on the economic impact of the decline of the fishing industry in the North of Scotland or the influence of traditional story telling on the development of modern Native American literature and you find a press with a regional or specialist interest in these areas. But if your book has a more general appeal and might have a market in both Europe and the US it probably makes more sense for you to go with one of the bigger, international players.

The American University Presses

One option that we haven't discussed yet which falls somewhere between the two extremes we have explored is that offered by the American University Presses. Thanks in part to the huge number of universities and academics to which it is home, the United States is uniquely blessed in having a large number of university presses, around 100 at the last count. So many are there they have their own association – the American Association of University Presses (AAUP). Founded in 1937 the AAUP lobbies on its members' behalf, carries out industry research and analysis, manages collaborative programs between presses and provides a number of useful services such as the 'Books For Understanding' section of their website which lists scholarly books on topics in the news and was very widely consulted in the aftermath of 9/11. If you think that your thesis might in any way appeal to an American market it would make a lot of sense to consider publishing with one of these presses, regardless of whether you are based in the US yourself. It is true that like most academic publishers that do not focus entirely on textbooks, many of these presses are struggling and a few have even gone under in the last few years due to the pressures discussed in Chapter 1. Many of them however benefit from substantial endowments or are subsidized by their parent universities. Yet others have diversified into other kinds of publishing such as local interest books covering regional flora and fauna, traditional cookery and local history which to some degree underwrite their academic programme. The bigger, more prestigious university presses will all be familiar names – Harvard, Yale, Princeton, Chicago, University of California – but there are also many mid-range presses such as Johns Hopkins, Duke, Cornell and New York University Press which have established enviable reputations in a number of fields and would be valuable additions to any CV.

Moving down the scale in terms of size but not quality there are also a substantial number of university presses that are well known and respected in a particular, specialist area, often due to a particularly active editor or series editor. University of Minnesota Press for instance has a long running series in Social Movements; Indiana University Press has a reputation for publishing cutting edge material in gay and lesbian studies; Temple University Press has strong programmes in Asian-American studies and sport and society (amongst other areas); – and so on. Publishing with one of the American University Presses that has a presence in your field could prove a smart move for many of the reasons we have already identified such as getting more attention and personalized guidance through the publishing process with a smaller organization, much to be desired for your first publishing experience. In addition, because of the sheer number of presses the odds of finding an editor ready and willing to take on your book are for once stacked in your favor.

Thinking about multiple markets: subjects and end-users

We have looked at the question of trying to find the publisher who can best reach the potential market for your book but what if your book is genuinely multidisciplinary, and for instance, addresses a topic that is in the intersection between political theory and social theory? It would then be worth looking to see if within your short-list of publishers specializing in political theory there was also one that had a strong list in sociology. Although publishers are wary of books that claim to be interdisciplinary or multidisciplinary, if there is a genuine case to be made that a book will appeal to more than one discipline publishers are generally keen to exploit synergies between lists and will make a real effort to ensure that the book is featured in all the relevant catalogs and websites and goes to all the appropriate conferences.

Thinking about the end-user or reader is essential when revising your thesis for publication but it is also important when thinking about publishers. As well as being identifiable by their particular disciplinary background most readers of academic books can also be divided into three types: students (undergraduate and graduate), academics, and professionals. The likelihood is that your book will be of interest to graduate students and academics but there are some areas such as developmental psychology, clinical psychology, criminology, business studies, and social work where there is clearly potential, on occasion, for crossover into a professional market. Not all academic publishers have the expertise or resources to target professional markets effectively so it is worth checking that your publisher of choice is able to if this is likely to be relevant to you. Only a few minutes research on their website or in their catalogs will quickly give you a sense of whether your chosen publisher is publishing books for professionals not only because they are mentioned as a group in marketing blurbs and publicity but also because professional books have a number of easily recognizable characteristics. They are expensive, often published in hardback or high priced paperback, have plain covers, titles that eschew the clever or the poetic, and make their publishers lots of money. Professional books provide their end-user with factual information and guidance on good practice. If they contain any theoretical material it will simply be as a framework for understanding or contextualizing said information and practice and will not be discussed in any great detail. It is therefore unlikely that a book based on your thesis will fall within the category of professional books though it is a market you should be aware of, especially if one day you are likely to work in the medical and allied health professions, management or law.

Production values

The final issue to consider when choosing your publisher may seem fairly trivial and inconsequential, especially when you are working hard to find a publisher and may on occasion feel grateful to anyone who takes the time to show an interest in you and your work. But good production values can play a significant part in the success or otherwise of your book. By good production values I mean a number of different but related things and here again, time spent carefully looking at books *en masse*, and individually, in bookshops and libraries will be of benefit to you. The physical look and feel of your book can be almost as important as its content if you are competing against a whole raft of other books on Virginia Woolf or globalization.

The initial and most immediate impact a book can make is through its cover and it is worth noting that you cannot expect to have a four color cover as a matter of course because they are expensive to produce and the publisher may well feel that the potential market for your book does not merit one. You can, however, expect to have an attractive and well-designed cover on which your name and the title of the book stand out clearly. The quality of the paper, the clearness of the printing, the strength of the binding, whether the pages stay open, page layout and design all play their part as well and will effect whether your book is a desirable object. And as discussed in Chapter 1, in a world where much research is available online there has to be a compelling reason for someone to pay good money to buy your book and for them to want to possess it as a thing in its own right. For them to pick it up, touch it, look at it, hold it, read and re-read it and want to keep it. Especially when the simple acquiring of information, often for free or at a relatively low cost, has become so easy that it can be digested and discarded when no longer of interest or use.

Good production values also manifest themselves in the quality of the copy editing and proofreading and if you are lucky enough to secure a publisher who takes both seriously (surprising though it may seem, this is not something you can always take for granted) then you and your book will benefit greatly. Even if you are not a student of style or particularly interested in grammar, or if English is not your first language, you can rest assured that if you have a good copy editor you will not be embarrassed and the reader will not be distracted by spelling mistakes, strange constructions and sentences that go nowhere. Similarly good proofreading will ensure that all the copy editor's corrections are made and that there are no annoying typographical mistakes. Good copy editing, typesetting and proofreading are particularly important if there are significant amounts of data in the form of figures, graphs and tables in your work or lots of equations. With so much of the production process being out-sourced these days it could easily be that the person working on your manuscript has no expertise in your subject area and is not a native English speaker, both of which factors can lead to new errors creeping into the text, a situation that you will wish to avoid if at all possible. Not only because it is immensely distressing to receive back proofs that are in a worse condition than the manuscript you originally submitted, but also because correcting them and ensuring that your corrections are fully incorporated in the final set of proofs is a lengthy and time-consuming process. So while poor production values can turn a good book into a bad one, careful copy editing and proofreading can help to turn a not so good book into a better one and help a first time author sound less like a first time author.

Are some publishers more prestigious than others?

This last question is very difficult to quantify or gain any objective measure of but it is undoubtedly true that some publishers enjoy a higher status than others. It is also true that there are very few publishers who are regarded as world leaders in every area they cover, so you need to take this into account too. These differences and indeed hierarchies of reputation may or may not be justified but they are a fact of life. I remember vividly several years ago telling a professor who was a series editor and senior university administrator that I was moving to a job at Cambridge University Press. He was delighted for me and congratulated me on the fact that I would now have the power to make or break academic careers. "Surely not!" I replied rather nervously. "But of course" he replied gravely "A young academic who has published with Cambridge has a much greater chance of securing tenure or a research grant than one who has published with a less prestigious publisher." Even if this was true in the past in some subject areas, it is certainly not true that editors have the power to influence individual careers nowadays and neither would they wish to. Most editors have more than enough to cope with trying to manage and develop financially viable and academically respectable lists. And being an academic editor is definitely not the obvious career choice for a megalomaniac! But there is a serious point in all this. Getting your PhD published is good but getting it published by a publisher that has a high reputation within your own academic community is even better. John Mullan, Professor of English Literature at University College, London makes the advantages of publishing with a leading academic publishing house very clear:

I first got published by OUP. The process took a very long time, but, in retrospect, I realised that having a book published by such a heavyweight press was a big advantage. It got substantial reviews in the *TLS* and *LRB*, it got into all the Faculty libraries – and it was well-produced and properly copy-edited. I think that the advocacy of my PhD supervisor – Tony Tanner – played a big part in getting OUP to look seriously at what I had done. The biggest advantage I had was a research fellowship, which gave me the time (almost a year) to rewrite every single sentence of the thesis. It now seems quite verbose to me, but at least it was written to be a book rather than a thesis.

There are no league tables for publishers – partly as we discussed before because publishers are constantly having to change and adapt and their current standing can be affected by their staff (the loss or acquisition of a particularly well-known and respected editor), current levels of investment and the vagaries of academic fashion. But it is worth bearing this whole question in mind when drawing up your shortlist and later on when you are discussing possible changes or revisions and negotiating terms. The most prestigious publishers in your field may not necessarily offer the best financial terms. They may also, as a result of their own reviewing processes ask you to make substantial revisions to your manuscript which you feel reluctant to do having already gone through a lengthy process of rewriting and revising your doctorate. On the other hand, less well-established publishers may offer you a higher royalty and be prepared to publish your thesis pretty much as is. It is quite possible, however, that the higher royalty is in reality a larger piece of a much smaller pie as their marketing and distribution operations are not as extensive and they skimp on copy editing and proofreading. Thus they have lower overheads and can afford to offer what are ostensibly higher payments on a poorly produced book which only reaches a small proportion of its potential market. I have to admit I am biased against this latter type of publishing and personally believe academic publishers are there to provide added value and quality to the books they produce but there is certainly a place for a less precious approach which sees speed to market as more important than a lengthy review process and a carefully coordinated marketing campaign. How you decide to balance short term advantage with longer term considerations will need to be informed by the demands of your subject as discussed in Chapter 2. Speed to market is obviously less of a consideration for historians than it is for research-orientated social scientists. The particular stage at which you are at in your career will also influence your decision: more specifically whether you have already secured a contract teaching or research position or even the Holy Grail of tenure. Whatever course you finally decide on, you should consider these issues carefully and remember that the best publishers in an area don't acquire their reputation by chance but from years of delivering consistently high quality books.

Should you approach more than one publisher at a time?

After an extensive research process, considering every aspect of the services a particular publisher can offer you, you will by now have arrived at a shortlist of publishers you would like to be published by. We will discuss the manner in which you make your approach in the next chapter but the final question that you may want to consider here is whether you should send out your sample material and proposal to all of them at the same time on a kind of scattergun principle, hoping that if you fire enough shots into the air one of them might hit the bull's eye. Or should you take a more carefully targeted approach, starting with the one you would most like to secure a contract from and not moving on to the next one on your list until you are certain that the previous option has been excluded? The answer is, as you may have already guessed, that there are no easy answers.

My feeling as a book publisher is that you should go for the latter option. My heart always sinks slightly when a proposal arrives with a note saying that the proposal has been sent to a number of different publishers as that immediately puts me under time pressure to secure reviews and arrive at a decision as to whether I want to make a formal offer in the first place. Then if the other publishers are also interested I will be under pressure to make an offer that at least matches or betters theirs. Being under pressure is of course part of any job and if a project is worth having it's worth fighting for. It does depend on the nature of the project though. If it is a major trade book or textbook or a groundbreaking monograph by a leading figure then I am quite prepared to put myself in a competitive situation. If it is for a revised PhD thesis I may well think twice about investing the time and money involved in a review process if there is a chance that I won't secure the project at the end of it, even if the reviews are positive. This may seem unfair but the reality is that I could be spending the same time and money developing a project I know I will see a return on and possibly a much larger return too. In other words as economists would say, the opportunity cost is too high. I would also wonder how much the potential author really wanted to be published by my company. If they do really want to be published by us as opposed to any one of a handful of publishers it is often an indicator that the author has done their research and that there will be a good marketing fit between our lists and their project. If they don't care who they are published by as long as they are published then it is a less attractive gamble.

However, and this is a big however, there are a number of arguments in favor of the scattergun approach and the truth is that I have never not reviewed a project I was genuinely interested in simply because it had been offered to another publisher. If there is any chance that your research might become out-of-date or be superseded you may not want to wait several months for one publisher to make up his or her mind before you set things in motion with another publisher, especially if the final answer is going to be a no. Even if this is not the case you may feel it is prudent not to put all your eggs in one basket. Not long ago I was discussing this very issue with an American professor who has used his power and influence to help and advise many young academics just starting on their publishing careers. He took the view that it was only reasonable for first time authors to approach a number of different publishers but it was imperative that they should be open about it and that once they had received an expression of interest from one publisher they should follow that and always be honest and not try to play different publishers off against each other. Such a sensible sounding view is hard to argue with. So perhaps the answer, as with so many things, is that it depends. It depends on whether you have a personal recommendation from a senior academic to a particular editor, in which case you should definitely follow that through before trying elsewhere. It also depends on how time-sensitive the material is and whether you can afford to wait (rather than simply being too impatient to wait). It depends in part on what the norms are in your particular discipline – and that is something else on which you could take advice from senior colleagues. It also depends on how you handle it and on whether you have the time, energy and juggling skills to keep several balls in the air at the same time and to follow up more than one expression of interest – if you find yourself in that lucky position – with tact and efficiency. Only you can be a judge of that.

To sum up:

- Do some research. Go to your library and your local campus bookshop. Look at the books in your area carefully for the information they can give you about different imprints and publishers and how well they produce their books.

- Do access publisher's websites, catalogs and conference exhibitions and talk to friends and colleagues about their own experiences and perceptions of different publishers.

- Do think about marketing fit. How well does your project fit different publishers' lists? How effectively can they reach the disciplinary and geographic markets you need to reach?

- Do think about production quality and added value.

- Do approach more than one publisher at a time if you have good reason to need a contract quickly but do be careful how you do it and always be honest about it.

- Don't just send your proposal out to the first few publishers that come to mind.

- Don't believe everything people tell you: sometimes they have their own reasons for criticizing a particular publisher.

- Don't forget to consider all aspects of the service a potential publisher has to offer, including electronic publication, marketing, sales and their reputation.

- Don't try to play publishers off against each other. They won't want to play and the world of academic publishing is a small one.

- Don't give up!

5

PREPARING AND PRESENTING A PROPOSAL

This chapter will provide basic guidance on putting together a proposal. It will cover everything from using the right kind of paper and font to making sure you provide all the necessary information at the appropriate level of detail. When to approach, who and how to approach, are all discussed as is following up your initial approach. Tailoring your proposal to individual publishers and the ideal covering letter are also covered.

To say that writing the perfect academic book proposal is an art form in itself may be the kind of exaggeration to which only those of us who read or write them on a regular basis are prone. In fact, when I tried to think of a perfect proposal to use as an example to include in this book I failed. And when I asked each of my colleagues if they could supply me with one they failed too, each one suggesting that I try another editor, in another discipline, as if it might exist somewhere but they had not personally come across it. Which is another way of saying that there may be a perfect, platonic form of the proposal but for our purposes all that matters is writing one good enough to secure an editor's attention. In order to do that you simply need to remember that a proposal is like any literary form or genre and has certain rules and conventions that if observed will substantially increase your chances of success and are ignored at your peril.

A book proposal is an advertisement and a story. It's aim is to engage the attention and to give an immediate sense of authority and control. It seeks to persuade the reader of the fascinating and original nature of its subject matter, the clarity and elegance of its style, and, most important of all, the quality of its scholarship. Anything that enhances and reinforces these properties is to be encouraged. Anything that detracts from them should be shunned.

Now that you have put together your short list of publishers and perhaps identified your first choice, this chapter will seek to guide you through the process of putting together a proposal, deciding what material to send with it and making your first contact. We will begin by looking at the basic rules you need to follow in order to put together a successful proposal. Many of them relate to issues of presentation but they also concern content, level and style. We will then explore the various ways in which you can adapt your proposal to suit the needs and tastes of different publishers and conclude by considering what should go in your covering letter and when the ideal time is to submit your proposal.

Putting together a proposal

Before you start writing your proposal the first thing you should do is look at the website of your favored publisher to establish what their preferences are with regard to the submission of manuscripts and proposals. When you have done so, it is worth trawling through the websites of a few other academic publishers as well just to get a sense of how these guidelines or requirements vary from publisher to publisher. You will soon notice that there is considerable variation and you need to be aware of this if you are going to submit your proposal to more than one publisher at a time – or indeed if you find that your first submission is not successful and you need to approach another publisher. Some require a proposal of no more than three–four pages long, while others set the limit at ten pages. Some are happy to receive as much draft material as you want to send them, while others very emphatically state 'No Manuscripts Please!' Some will only accept electronic submissions and others will only accept hard copy.

All of them, however, are remarkably consistent in terms of what they require a proposal to cover, even though they may differ slightly in the way they express it and the terms they use. The clear consensus is that a proposal should include the following elements:

1 *Rationale/overview/statement of aims*
  Whatever you choose to call this section of the proposal, it is the most important part of the whole thing and where you will generally win or lose your prospective editor. Like a good book blurb it has to draw the reader in and make them want to learn more. It is therefore worth taking time over it and working through several drafts. Try it out on friends who may or may not know anything about the subject matter but will be able to tell you if it sounds as if it makes sense and flows smoothly and logically. Don't assume a tone which is overly familiar and casual but equally do try to avoid sounding pompous and overblown. Simplicity is the key and you will do yourself no favours if you try to oversell your project at this stage. You need to clearly state the aims and objectives of the book, tell the reader what it is about, what approach you have taken and why, and your reasons for wanting to write this book now. You should also explain very clearly how your book relates to the existing literature and what contribution it would hope to make to that literature. This last should enable the editor to immediately contextualize your proposal so that they can tell at a glance what its subject matter is and how it might fit into their list. At some point, either at the end of the rationale or in your covering letter you will need to give an indication of the nature of the revisions you will be undertaking to transform your thesis into a book, whether you have started the revisions process and if so how far you have progressed with it. It is difficult to say exactly how long the rationale section should be but I would say you will need at least two pages to do justice to your project and cover all the items listed above but more than five pages and the editor will lose patience or get distracted by something else.

2 *Table of contents*
  This should include a list of chapter headings and a paragraph or two on each chapter covering key ideas and themes. You do not want to get bogged down with too much detail in producing these summaries

but rather concentrate on conveying the scope or range of the material you intend to cover and emphasizing what is original or different about your treatment of it. If you remember to include a preface and acknowledgements at the beginning and index and bibliography/references at the end it will make it look more professional.

3 *Reader/market*
This section is actually much trickier than it sounds. If you claim that the book will appeal to everyone in your own discipline, cognate disciplines and that mythical beast 'the interested reader' you will give the editor the definite impression that you do not know what you are talking about. On the other hand if you are too cautious (others might say honest) and suggest that the book might only be of interest to the handful of scholars (specializing for instance, in the railway as social and economic metaphor in the nineteenth century American novel), you have effectively removed any incentive for the editor to exercise their innate optimism and believe that the book might sell more than 200 copies in its entire life. In a case such as this you should draw attention to the core market for the book but defined in its broadest terms – scholars and students of the nineteenth century American novel – and a feasible additional or supplementary market, perhaps economic and social historians. In the rare event that your book genuinely would appeal across a number of disciplines either because your area of research is inherently multidisciplinary, such as gender studies, or you have taken on a large, ambitious topic such as the evolutionary development of language, you will need to clearly identify and distinguish between key and additional markets. As the evolutionary development of language is such a large and important area of research you might simply put that as your key market and then, depending on your own disciplinary background and approach, put evolutionary psychology, cognitive science, linguistics and neurobiology in varying combinations after it. If your book is based around original ethnographic research you have carried out on a group of 18 young women of Asian descent exploring their experience of work and discrimination (for example), the book could technically be of interest to scholars of gender studies, Asian studies, ethnographic studies, cultural anthropology, sociology of work, employment studies, race and ethnicity

studies and youth studies. I hope, however, that by now it will be obvious that such a large and undiscriminating list is counterproductive and that rather than convincing the editor that there are lots of potential markets for your book it is more likely to make them fear that it will slip between the proverbial stools. With books such as these it is essential that you take a long hard look at what is distinctive and original about your work and target it towards one or two key markets rather than try, and inevitably fail, to appeal to all. One final note on the difference between readership and market, though these terms are often used interchangeably, generally readership signifies the type of reader and level – researcher, graduate, lecturer – and market, the discipline, and geographic appeal.

4 *Competition*
Even if you are genuinely convinced, hand on heart, that your book is unique and that there is not now, nor ever will be, a book to compare with it, to put 'None' under the heading 'competition' looks like you simply aren't trying – or, even worse, that you are not familiar with the literature. Given that you and your supervisor probably spent quite a long time in the initial stages of your PhD trying to find a suitably distinctive and original take on your chosen subject, the chances are there is no other book on exactly the same topic. But this, paradoxically, is not necessarily a good thing. It may be it is generally considered too narrow an area/perspective/ approach to justify and sustain a book length treatment. Hopefully this is something you will have thought carefully about during the course of reading Chapters 2 and 3, and having decided that a book is the right format in which to publish your work, your task is to convince editor and reviewers your book will fill a real gap in the literature not only by describing what it is, which you will have done in the rationale, but also by defining what it is not, in the section on competition. So unless your chosen topic is a very broad one and there are lots of other books on general equilibrium theory (for example), you are safest saying there is no direct competition but then listing those books which come closest to yours in terms of scope and approach and explaining how yours differs from them. Perhaps they cover a narrower or a broader range, are more or less theoretical in approach, or take a very specific line of argument. Only list those books which really are relevant though:

listing every single book published on the topic in the last few years will not endear you to the reader/editor. While demonstrating that you have a secure command of search engines, it won't help the reader/ editor to get a real sense of your book and place it in context if you overburden them with too much information. On the other hand you should take good care to include those key books which are published by the editors you are approaching to show that you are aware of their publishing programme and have thought about how your book might fit in with it. It is probably prudent not to be too rude about these, even if in your opinion they are not very good. Indeed it is wise not to be too harsh about any of the books you include in this section. While a more established scholar may get away with making provocative comments about another's work, a younger scholar may be challenging but can never afford to be seen to be arrogant or dismissive.

5　Finally it is worth having a short section at the end of the proposal which indicates your expected delivery date, proposed length in thousands of words or pages, and the number of figures and tables and any illustrated material you are hoping to use, including photographs and maps. Try to make this as accurate as possible but do bear in mind that the more illustrations you use and the greater the length, the more expensive the book will be to produce. This will inevitably impact on the editor's decision as to whether to pursue the project further both from a point of view of cost and potential hassle quotient. If they are prepared (as many are not) to take a punt on a revised PhD thesis, the very last thing they will want to risk is a project that is going to take up a lot of their time. If they think that there will be lots of production issues such as checking whether permissions have been sought or deciding whether figures and tables will need re-drawing they are likely to beat a hasty retreat. One way around this which has become increasingly popular in the last few years, is to put material that is expensive to reproduce or is likely to date on a dedicated website that you would maintain and update but could be linked directly to the publisher's own web pages. You will obviously need to have a web page of your own that you can use in this way and/or the necessary skills to set one up (or someone willing to help you) but you do not need to go into very much detail at this stage. The important thing is to indicate your willingness to do this if the publisher deems it appropriate and then you can discuss it with friends and colleagues once the book is accepted and with the administrators of your institution's website in due course. There are also plenty of good books and manuals available to help you if you are not lucky enough to find someone to do it for you.

The Covering Letter

The perfect covering letter should, in my opinion, be short, clear and to the point. Whether its physical form is that of an email message or an actual piece of paper, it is vital to your chances of success that the editor reading it can tell at a glance (a) what you are asking them to do (consider your proposal for review), (b) what it is about (is it a subject they might be interested in?), and (c) who you are.

This last may seem rather unnecessary; surely an academic publisher only deals with academics? But over the years I have received emails and book proposals from every kind of person. A Greek plumber with a general theory of human relationships based on his experience of the divorcee dating scene; an ex-Indian railway worker with a plan for transforming the Indian economy, a depressed housewife who described in vivid detail the isolation of living on a modern executive housing estate. All of these letters and proposals need to be read, acknowledged and dealt with and put in one pile or another. Bearing in mind that the average academic editor receives at least one unsolicited proposal a day (which may not sound like a lot but quickly mounts up) it is imperative that you do everything you can to help them identify your project as a serious one that is worth considering rather than another one to add to the pile to be graciously but firmly declined.

Addressing your letter

As I write this book I am aware that to the educated and sophisticated audience to whom it is addressed some of the advice it contains may seem simplistic, even banal. But let me assure you, my own experience suggests that this is not the case, even with the most basic things like addressing your letter to the right person or right publisher. Mistakes tend to happen most frequently with letters that are produced on a computer and sent out with multiple submissions so if you do decide to take this approach, check and check again before sealing and addressing your envelopes. I know for a fact that I am not the only publisher to have received a letter addressed inside the envelope to another publisher and containing fulsome praise of a competitor's list! While everyone understands that accidents happen and that human beings are fallible, it is hard to recover from such a mistake. Though I try not to let it influence my judgment of the project in question, it inevitably colors my perception of the person or people involved, not least raising doubts about their attention to detail and their organizational skills. And in a difficult and competitive climate the very last thing that you want to do with your covering letter is create new hurdles for yourself to overcome in the effort to get your project sent out for review, let alone offered a contract.

So check and double check your letter or email are addressed to the right publisher before you send it and make the effort to find out the relevant editor's name. Given that nearly all publishers nowadays have extensive websites listing commissioning editors with full contact details and areas of responsibility, not to find out and use the editor's name is sheer laziness and creates a sense of distance and lack of engagement which is unlikely to encourage the serious consideration of your project. Use their name in full (Dear Sarah Caro) and do not assume the editor's gender especially if they have a name (such as Pat or Chris) which is not gender specific. Do not use any title (Dear Dr Caro) unless one is listed on the website.

Having steered your way safely through the surprisingly perilous course of name and address, it is essential, as discussed earlier, to establish your credentials right at the start of your communication. This can be done either by stating your affiliation and position or by mentioning the name of the established academic/author who has recommended that you write to this particular publisher. So you might begin:

I am an assistant professor of political science at the University of Aalborg

Or

I am a research fellow at the Yerkes Primate Research Center and I am writing to you at the suggestion of Professor Isabella Sutton to ask if you might be interested in...

This is even more important if you are sending an email rather than a letter as you do not have the benefit of visual signifiers such as headed notepaper or postmarks which will prime the busy editor that this is a bona fide project. In addition you are also battling against a huge tide of spam and unsolicited emails of which only the first few lines may be read, if they are opened at all. Having established that you are not a crank and that you have a serious academic background, the next task is to describe your project as briefly and succinctly as you can at the same time as providing enough detail to interest the editor reading your letter and make them want to learn more – by reading your proposal. The editor needs to feel this is an interesting topic, that you know what you are talking about and that there is a possibility it might fit into their current publishing program. Only then will they invest the time and energy necessary to give your proposal a thorough read through and consider sending it out for review.

As well as covering all of the necessary information it is important to get the right tone in your letter and strike a happy balance between enthusiasm and effusiveness on the one hand, and realism and negativity on the other. I recently received a letter from an American professor concerning a major research project she wanted to write up and turn into a book. It went something like this:

Dear Editor

I have been involved for the past five years with a wonderful group of people on a truly original project. It has been an enormously fruitful and fulfilling collaborative experience for us all and we have collected a huge amount of data and are now ready to write a book. We are sure that you too will feel this is a worthwhile endeavour and will want to help us reach the large number of people at all levels and across a wide range of disciplines who will want to know about our work. ...

Now allowing for the fact that I am a curmudgeonly old Brit, the fact is there is no reason at all for me to be interested in whether you have had a personally fulfilling experience doing your research or whether you even liked your colleagues. What I might be interested in is the project itself but as you will have noticed, in the whole of that first paragraph there is nothing to say in what discipline the work is rooted, the name of the institution where it was carried out, the names or experience of the people involved or the topic of the proposed book. Letters like this are a turn-off. While the author may think they are conveying enthusiasm and all manner of positive qualities they actually sound rather self-satisfied and are wasting an editor's precious time because they have not given sufficient thought to what they needed to say. They have a good chance of being rejected. Equally certain of rejection but a rejection that comes in sadness rather than irritation are those letters which paint an overly gloomy picture of the task ahead. Another recent letter from a young academic in search of a contract read as follows:

Dear Editor

I am writing to ask if you would consider my PhD for publication. I realize that turning my thesis into a book will be a long and difficult process but I am willing to take your advice on what needs to be done and to work as hard as necessary to achieve this challenging goal.

This letter makes you feel weary and overwhelmed by the task ahead before you even hear what the proposed project is. The author's intentions are good – they are clearly trying to indicate that they are aware a thesis is not the same as a book and that they will need to revise it substantially before publication. However they are also indicating that they have not yet begun any of this work and will require an awful lot of input and handholding that the editor probably doesn't have the time or sufficient incentive to offer. In effect they have dissuaded any editor from wanting to take on the project in their very first paragraph. Both of these examples clearly illustrate the point that you should always try to imagine how you might respond if you received such a letter from someone you didn't know. While editors are predisposed to give you the benefit of the doubt, they are only human.

If you are writing to an editor with a recommendation (either written or verbal) from an established academic you should think of it as a letter of introduction rather than a guarantee of publication. Another letter I once received is a good example of how not to use such a recommendation.

Dear Sarah Caro

I am writing to you because Professor Alvarez thought you might be interested in publishing my thesis Identity and Gender in a Post Foucauldian World. Here it is. Please let me know if you decide to publish.

Yours sincerely
Ann Autre

Hopefully you will immediately see what is wrong with this letter. The assumption behind it is that the recommendation from Professor Alvarez is enough to secure consideration of the project. There is no attempt to tell me about the project, to interest me in it (apart from mentioning the professor's name), or to indicate that the author is aware that it will need work to turn it into a book and if so whether they have undertaken any revisions. Clearly I don't have time to read through the whole manuscript on the off chance that it might be of interest. I am either going to turn it down there and then or out of respect and consideration for the academic who has recommended the project I will have to get back to them and reluctantly ask them for a full proposal. Reluctantly as it is clear from this letter that the person involved has not thought very carefully about the process and is going to be a nightmare to work with if the project is worth taking on!

The letter they should have written would have started something like this;

Dear Sarah Caro

I am writing at the suggestion of Professor Alvarez to ask if you might be interested in considering my book Identity and Gender in a Post Foucauldian World which builds on my doctoral thesis. I was awarded my doctorate at the University of California, Davis in 2007 (where I am now working as an assistant professor) and Professor Alvarez was one of my external reviewers. I have attached a brief proposal and table of contents and would be grateful if you could let me know if this is something you might be interested in discussing further.

Note that I have suggested that the writer refer to it as their book rather than their PhD. Of course you cannot pretend the book is other than it is, a re-working of your thesis. But if you refer to it only as your PhD you are immediately setting off alarm bells in the prospective editor's mind that you have not thought about the process of transforming your thesis into a book and that it will demand a great deal of time and effort to turn it into something that is publishable. You are likely to be politely reminded that dissertations and books are very different, that they are written for different purposes and that whatever the subject, however interesting and original the research, the publisher you have approached never publishes theses as they are and please go away and don't come back until you have rewritten it. That's if you are lucky and the editor you have contacted is conscientious, in a good mood and is vaguely interested in having something in this area. If you are not lucky you will just get the standard 'sorry we don't publish PhD's' line. By describing it as a book, however, 'building' on your doctoral research or 'originating' from that research you are making it clear to the editor that you know the score. You are signaling your tacit understanding that they will not want to consider an unrevised PhD but that they might consider a project in which the original research or theoretical work is restructured, re-organized and expanded and developed to make it into a work that might be of interest to fellow researchers and academics in the area.

Finally close your letter by making it clear that you have not chosen to approach this particular publisher at random, but because you admire and are familiar with their list and think that your book would complement their current publishing programme. Excessive flattery or obsequiousness are definitely a turn-off but the odd compliment or word of appreciation never did any harm. Nor does the sense that you have chosen that particular publisher over the others you could have written to (more of which in a moment).

After your signature make sure that you include your email address and that somewhere on the letter – exactly where will obviously vary depending on whether it is a hard copy or email – all of your contact details are easily accessible.

Less is more

As you may have noticed, all the advice I have given so far is designed to help you give your project credibility and to emphasize your academic credentials. Do not be tempted to undermine this good work in an effort to make your proposal distinctive or stand out from the slush pile for any other reason than its intellectual quality or originality. Coloured paper, multi-coloured text, fancy formatting and exotic fonts are all a no-no. Your word processing skills are of absolutely no interest to the editor and you run the risk of producing something that looks like an end of term school project rather than a serious academic work. If your material contains significant amounts of quantative data then do of course include some sample figures or tables but remember that the way in which you use and analyze the material they contain is more important to the editor and potential reviewer than their formatting. (This is because many publishers will have figures professionally redrawn anyway before typesetting.) Use plain paper if you are submitting hard copy, black type and a clear font such as Times New Roman or Arial for either hard or electronic copy as they are clear, easy-to-read and won't distract from the content.

Adapting your proposal for different publishers

As I have already mentioned in this chapter and in chapter 4 it is highly advisable to adapt your proposal and covering letter wherever possible to the needs and interests of the various publishers to whom you will be sending them. Though this will involve some extra work on your part and while there are, of course, no guarantees in this business, the chances are that your efforts will be amply rewarded in terms of the seriousness and interest with which the editor views your project.

So how do you go about the process of adaptation? Well the important thing to remember is that it does not need to be a dramatic or drastic process. An additional tweak here, a couple of extra sentences there, are probably all that will be needed to make the editor feel that this has been a carefully planned and executed approach and to ensure you a sympathetic reading. Getting the address right and finding out the appropriate editor's name are, as already discussed, essential in the covering letter as is signaling your familiarity with their publishing programme. The rationale section of your proposal also provides an excellent opportunity to explain just how your book would complement the editor's existing list and by mentioning comparable titles and possible series within which your book might be included, you are making it easier for the editor to see just how your project might work for them by plugging a gap here or helping to build up a new area of interest there. Adapting your proposal like so much of the publishing process is about trying to see your 'baby', your special project into which you have put so much time and energy, from an outsider's perspective. Not necessarily an objective perspective but one which comes with a different set of pressures and preconceptions. Anything that you can do that shows your awareness of these pressures will enhance your chances of getting published and will enable you to make your initial approach and follow up in a way that maximizes the chances of it being favourably considered.

Making Contact and Following Up

Having completed your proposal and covering letter and found out the name of the relevant editor/editors you are ready to make your initial approach but this, like everything else needs a little thought and forward planning. There are certain times of year when editors are less likely to be in the office and your proposal has an increased chance of languishing at the bottom of a rapidly filling intray/box. This is not only annoying as you are likely to spend several frustrating weeks waiting with no news of your project but it is also a positive disadvantage as it removes all sense of urgency for the editor. If a project has come in while they were away on business or on vacation and was not sufficiently important for their assistant to deal with or draw to their attention then the natural tendency, I would suggest, is to think that a few days more won't make much difference. And then as the editor struggles to catch up with the administrative jobs that have built up and urgently need their attention, to follow up on their trip if they were away on business, and to respond to the new demands on their time constantly coming from outside, the days will turn into weeks until about a month after their return they will finally make their way to the bottom of the intray or to that last email message. They will take a quick look at the proposal and look at the date and partly out of embarrassment that it has taken them so long to respond, partly because it no longer seems fresh and exciting, and partly because they will assume that if it was any good it has already gone to another publisher, they will write a quick note of rejection and move on to the next job.

This is of course a worst case scenario but I would be willing to bet that every academic editor, however efficient and conscientious, has been in this position at least once and written a hasty letter of rejection because the timing wasn't right and they didn't have sufficient time and energy to consider it properly. So while timing is not all in this instance, it can be a significant factor. Which begs the question, when is a good time? Clearly the middle of the summer is NOT a good time. People go on vacation with families and friends. There are many conferences held during the summer months. And while it used to be a time when things eased off a little in the office and the pace of work noticeably slackened, changing timetables and working patterns, constant access to email, earlier starts to the academic year, have all ensured that this is no longer the case and the level of work carries on throughout the year at the same relentless rate. Easter is also a busy conference time and many publishers close down for at least part of the time over Christmas and New Year. Which leaves the first part of the year up to Easter, early summer (May, June), and September until the end of the year as prime times to send in proposals. You should also think about when the main events in your academic calendar are and bear in mind that if there are conferences, symposia and lecture series you are interested in, there is a possibility that an editor commissioning in your area might be engaged in them too. As I have said many times before in this book if you follow the general principles and guidelines suggested here, there are of course no guarantees but you will at least side step the most obvious pitfalls.

Following up

Once you have finally sent your proposal out into the big bad world the worst part of the process begins: waiting. If you are anything like me you will want an answer yesterday. You will find waiting for any kind of a decision or response that affects you closely, but over which you have no influence or control, torture. Excruciating. Almost unbearable. But be patient. Try to put it out of your mind and concentrate on something else for a few weeks. I know from experience that this is easier said than done but you should not expect an instant response and if you do receive one straight away the chances are it will be a quick decline. It is not impossible than an editor will see your proposal and be instantly inspired to contact you to discuss it further and to let you know they intend to send it out for review. It is, however, unlikely. It is much more likely that an experienced editor will immediately identify those projects which they do not feel are of a sufficiently high standard to consider or are in subject areas they are not interested in but will take longer to make a decision about those which are on a good topic but by an inexperienced author or clearly show their origins as PhD theses but nonetheless have something original to offer. In order to make a decision in such cases the editor may well want to consult their advisors, usually senior academics with whom they have a good relationship and know from experience will deliver a rapid but informed response which may well confirm the editor's initial instincts about the project. On the basis of these advisors' recommendations the editor will then decide whether to send the project out for review or tactfully turn it down, perhaps with some feedback on how the project might be improved before submitting to a more appropriate publisher.

So you should wait patiently for the publisher to get back to you but if you receive no acknowledgement that they have received your proposal and a month or more passes with no news, what do you do then? That is another of the key questions in this whole process to which it is very hard to give a definitive answer. So much depends on the publishing house and the editor. As we saw earlier in the section on putting together a proposal, publishing houses have surprisingly varied requirements in terms of what they expect to be covered in a proposal (indeed whether they will consider a proposal at all or only want to see manuscripts) and how they wish it to be submitted, so it is reasonable to suppose that they will have different attitudes to prospective authors following up their submissions. Editors also vary enormously in their responses to being chased and these responses will inevitably be colored not only by their own workloads and whatever other pressures they are under at the time but also by the style and tone of the chasing. Some editors will respond well to a gentle reminder and will not mind having their attention redirected to a project which they had perhaps put to one side while they dealt with more pressing issues. Others will find it an irritation and respond negatively. These differences in temperament or personality are unpredictable and unless you have inside information, unknowable. What you do have control over is the style and manner of your follow up. Writing another letter is usually a waste of time as it constitutes yet another piece of paper for the editor to deal with and will just be added to the pile. Telephoning is a high risk strategy. Some editors will find a telephone call an unforgivable intrusion on their time and resent the feeling that they are being put under pressure. Others may respond more positively especially if you strike the right note and manage to enquire after your project without sounding reproachful or impatient. Saying that you are calling just to check that they have received your proposal and to ask if there is any further information you can provide is your safest bet. Pressing them to decide whether they will review your proposal there and then is not advisable. Probably the safest strategy is a brief but friendly follow-up email. You do run the risk of it being ignored but it is the least intrusive means available to you and editors are generally pretty good at keeping up with their emails and responding relatively quickly.

To sum up:

- Do check the websites of the publishers you are planning to send your proposal to and find out their requirements and the name of the relevant editor.

- Do make sure your covering letter and proposal are clear and to the point by running them past a friend or colleague before you send them out.

- Do check and check again when you are sending out letters and proposals. Sending the wrong letter to the wrong editor makes a very bad initial impression that it's hard to recover from.

- Do think about timing. Try to avoid making your initial approach at a time when people are likely to be away on vacation or at the same time as major conferences in your subject area.

- Do be positive, concise and friendly in any further communication you have with the editor. They may not publish your first book but they might publish your second!

- Don't use colored paper, fancy fonts or excessive formatting as you risk your letter and proposal looking amateurish and childish.

- Don't make exaggerated claims for your own book: a realistic appraisal of the potential market for your book is much more likely to impress and give the impression you know what you are talking about.

- Don't be rude about the competition. Constructive criticism and comparison is ok if done in a measured way, but in excess it's not nice and people won't want to work with you.

- Don't despair if you don't hear back straight away. It may just be that the editor is taking the time to consider your proposal seriously.

- Don't be impatient or aggressive or sound aggrieved when and if you do decide to follow up. Your best course is to be pleasant, positive and persistent.

6

SURVIVING THE REVIEWS

This chapter outlines the benefits of the peer review process and how it works in most scholarly publishing houses. As well as discussing what you can do to help your proposal move as smoothly as possible through the process, it also considers the options available to you when the process appears to be delayed or collapse. What form the reviews are likely to take and the best way to respond when they finally arrive are also covered. Finally it looks at strategies for coping with rejection.

Of all the stages involved in getting an academic book published, the reviewing process is the most burdensome and frustrating for author and editor alike. Setting up suitable reviews for a proposal can take even the most experienced editor hours of work. While for an author, waiting for reviews is a bit like a cross between waiting to hear if you have got your first choice of university place and anticipating root canal surgery. Yet the review process is also the most important, and potentially, the most useful and rewarding stage of the publishing process (short of actually holding your new book in your hand). Without the system of (largely anonymous) peer review the major academic publishers would struggle to justify and maintain their existence.

As we saw in Chapter 4, publishers can add value to your manuscript with expert copy editing and production values. As we will see in Chapter 8, they can help you to reach a wider audience through the knowledge and expertise of their sales and marketing teams. But without the review process there would be little to distinguish them from the plethora of publishing outlets that became available first through on-demand, and then electronic and online publishing. Reviled and railed against as it sometimes is for being slow or unfair or reinforcing the established hegemony, the review process ensures certain standards of quality and scholarship. It also contributes in a small but significant way to the circulation of ideas at a relatively early stage in their development within a particular knowledge community. This can happen in a number of different ways. Firstly, if a reviewer is commissioned to look at a piece of work that they might not ordinarily have come across for a number of months/years, the process may directly or indirectly influence the reviewer's own research. It may confirm their belief that a certain topic has been and still is neglected or conversely that here is yet another book in an area that they were thinking of writing on and that their energies might be better directed elsewhere. Secondly, most academic publishers worth their salt will have a much larger, more international, and more varied pool of potential reviewers to call upon than the average academic has contacts, so they may well bring your work to the attention of scholars who would not otherwise hear of it. Thirdly by acting as a professional intermediary the publisher removes much of the stress and potential embarrassment for both author and reviewer. If an editor approaches a potential reviewer and requests their assistance there is little pressure either way and they will say yes if they are interested and no if they are too busy. A refusal is a nuisance but nothing more for the editor and they will simply try someone else. For an academic to approach a personal friend or colleague much more is at stake on both sides. If the friend/colleague says no they may cause offence, if they say yes they may also cause offence if they disagree with or criticize the work too strongly. All of which confirms the great virtues of the anonymous review system used by the majority of academic presses. It enables the reviewer to express their views honestly and openly without fear of hurting feelings, engaging in politics or risking friendships. It contributes to the maintenance of high quality scholarship and the development and dissemination of knowledge.

Of course no system however good is completely invulnerable to abuse. Occasionally reviewers hide behind their anonymity to vent their spleen but most experienced editors will be able to make a judgment call and either edit out those parts of the review which are gratuitously insulting or, in exceptional circumstances, withhold the review completely if they believe (after consulting with trusted advisors) that they have inadvertently unleashed a long standing personal or professional feud.

The review process in action

Having, I hope, established the many potential advantages of the process of anonymous peer review, there remains the question of how it actually works in practice. It would be disingenuous for me to pretend that it always works perfectly, that it is always an efficient system and that the reports received are always as conscientious and as helpful as one would wish. As I have outlined above, however, I do believe it is the best method available for judging the merits of a piece of work and ensuring the maintenance of academic standards. Given this and given the centrality of the review process to your chances of getting your thesis published it is worth spending a little time at this stage to explore some of the factors that influence the way the process is managed and the editor's choice of reviewers so that you can better understand it and possibly intervene if things do go wrong. Though intervention must always be a last resort and brings with it many caveats that we will address later.

For now let us assume things are proceeding well. The editor you approached liked your carefully crafted proposal and covering letter and thinks that your proposed book could be 'interesting' (a term all editors over-use mercilessly). They tell you they will set up some reviews and take it from there. This sounds simple enough but in reality commissioning reviews is the most time consuming and unpredictable of activities. Very occasionally you and the editor will be lucky and the first few people they approach will all say yes to the commission and the proposed timeframe straight away. More often than not though, it may take hours, days and even weeks to find reviewers who are qualified and willing to undertake the review, especially at certain times of year (as we discussed in the previous chapter).

But how does the editor decide who to approach? This is as important a question as it is difficult to answer for all editors and in all circumstances but undoubtedly it involves a combination of experience, pragmatism, and creativity. First of all a good editor relies on their understanding of the way a subject or discipline is structured. While they do not have to be experts or scholars themselves, they do need to know enough about the key people who have influenced the development of a discipline and those who are currently working in the field to choose reviewers who are suitably qualified to carry out the review. Most important of all, as a result of commissioning reviews over several years an editor will build up an extensive database (either in their heads or on computer) of the reviewers they have already used including information such as who is conscientious, who is not; who delivers when they say they will and who does not; and which reviewers tend to be excessively critical and which tend to give potential authors the benefit of the doubt. This database will also include the names of the authors they have already published, a good source of potential reviewers as they are all people known and trusted, who have been through the process themselves and know not only the process but also the requirements and preferences of that particular list or editor.

The fact that reviewers are commissioned on the basis of their knowledge of the material covered in the proposal may be self-evident and that editors tend to use people who are known and trusted should not be a surprise either but another factor which you may not have allowed for at this stage but can significantly impact on the review process, is timing. Not the kind of timing discussed in the last chapter which concerned external factors such as holidays and conferences but time pressures imposed by the internal workings of the publishing house. Most editors will be working towards a schedule or timetable dictated on the one hand by whether the editor has to take new proposals before a commissioning committee to be approved, and on the other by the requirements of their annual commissioning targets. There can be significant variations between publishing houses as to how the commissioning process is managed. Most will circulate internally some form of publishing proposal written by the editor including a brief description and rationale for publishing the book, copies of the reviews and a financial working. For some presses this is enough and as long as all the relevant people agree a contract can be offered at any time and there are no time constraints on the editor. If however, having been circulated internally, it is required that the papers

HOW TO PUBLISH YOUR PhD

are brought before a commissioning committee which may include people from outside the press who only meet at certain times of year, there are significant pressures upon the relevant editor to complete the review process within a specific timeframe so that they can hit the submission dates for those meetings. This is especially true of both Oxford and Cambridge University Presses which have commissioning boards (respectively known as the Delegates and the Syndics) composed largely of academics from the two universities who only meet every two weeks during term time. This system means that even though both presses have fast tracking procedures which can be invoked in special circumstances, in practice it means it is difficult for an editor to secure approval for a contract during the three to four months a year which fall outside term time.

Similarly, if an editor's budget year runs from January to December there will be a lot less pressure (and incentive) to get a proposal submitted in January reviewed, than one submitted in November. Not only because the editor has the whole year to process it and add it to their revenue but also because they are less likely to be anxious about hitting their targets.

Both types of time constraints can impact directly on the choice of reviewer. Professor Smith may be the world expert on Ovid (for example) but if the editor knows that he is always massively over-committed and is likely to take many months to provide a review which probably won't be very detailed, they may decide to ask someone who is less illustrious but more likely to deliver a useful review on time. An alternative strategy, if the editor is fairly confident that the proposal is worth pursuing, may be to seek a speedier response by asking three or four reviewers to provide brief comments rather than commission two longer reports which may take twice as long to arrive.

The final factor which can affect the choice of reviewer is the editor's perception of the potential market for a book. If the editor feels that there may be a market for the book in say both the US and Europe they will want to commission reviews from people based in both prospective markets so that they can confirm or otherwise that hunch and promote the book accordingly. Likewise, if they believe that there may be a cross disciplinary market for the book they will want to commission reviewers from within both the relevant disciplines. If your book attempts to appeal to several disciplines across a variety of geographic markets you may be in for a long and complex review process!

Once the editor has decided on and secured the potential reviewers, you may be wondering what kind of questions s/he is likely to ask them to address. I suspect this may have changed over the years and while intellectual originality and the potential contribution of the project to the literature may have been the main preoccupation in the past, editors nowadays will be equally concerned with the reviewer's assessment of the potential market for the book. This is summarized well in some guidelines I found that had been put together by one of my predecessors at OUP:

> All proposals for academic and college books to be published by Oxford University Press are considered by the Delegates of the Press (a committee of senior university academics). The Delegates' criteria for acceptance are stringent, and the likely demand for a book and its potential usefulness may need to be taken into account as well as its purely academic quality. We should be grateful therefore for your expert assessment of the enclosed proposal in two main areas – content and likely audience.

At the same time the editor will also be keen to ensure that they are contemplating a viable project that is reasonably well written and well structured and will not need a vast amount of work to turn it into a publishable book. This point is also succinctly covered in the guidelines:

> If it is apparent that this proposal will make a useful book then it is hoped that your comments about content and organization may help the author to improve the work. Accordingly we would like to be able to relay parts of your review to the author (while maintaining your anonymity). If you would prefer that your comments are not relayed to the author, or you do not mind the author knowing your identity, please indicate this at the end of your report.

Moving from the general to the more particular the specific questions the reviewers are asked to address will be something like those listed below:

1 Is the proposal likely to be a significant contribution to its field in presenting original material and/or an original argument? Does the organization of the book seem sensible? Is the choice and balance of topics appropriate and up to date?

2 Are there any subjects or topics not covered which in your opinion would form a necessary part of the book with this title and for this expected audience? Is there any material that you consider superfluous? Is the level appropriate?

3 Is there any significant overlap with books already published or known to be in preparation? Does this proposal look to be a good addition to the literature in this area?

4 Do you know the authors or editors as authorities in the field and do you feel that they are competent?

5 What is your assessment of the main readership for the book? Would it be of international interest?

If the editor is particularly worried about the exact nature and size of the possible market they might also include some more detailed questions such as 'would the potential sale be mainly to libraries or to individuals?'; or 'Would the book be of value to those who are not specialists in the subject?'; or even 'Would you buy it in book form or recommend your library or students to buy it?' But it is unusual for reviewers of academic monographs to be asked so specifically about the type of sales that might be expected, though if they are especially enthusiastic they may well proffer the information that if the book was published they would buy it!

If the discipline within which you are working requires the use of a significant amount of technical data, equations or mathematical proofs the reviewer may also be asked to check their accuracy. The stringency of the checking process at this stage may vary considerably from publisher to publisher and editor to editor, so the reviewer may be asked to work through every equation or only spot check the data and methods used, with a more thorough check being carried out later if the proposal is accepted for publication.

At the end of the list of points to be addressed the reviewer may be asked explicitly for their recommendation as to whether to publish or not. In the aforementioned guidelines they are asked:

> Do you recommend pursuing this proposal to publication, either in its present form or with the modifications you suggest, or should we decline this proposed book?

Some editors, however, are reluctant to state the question so plainly, in case they decide to go against the reviewer's judgment or in case reviewers are tempted to provide a simple yes or no response for the whole review, rather than elaborating on the reasons for their pronouncement, both of which circumstances could prove tricky in the advent of a negative decision.

The report that finally comes to you may well consist of simple bullet points addressing the questions raised but if you are lucky you will receive a detailed and engaged review that may run to several pages. Though this is not always the case, my experience has been that reviewers are often more conscientious about reviewing younger academics' work than that of their peers and that they are very aware of their responsibility to the next generation of scholars. Whether their final recommendation is to publish or not they will generally put serious thought into analysing both the strengths and weaknesses of the piece. The number of reports you receive will also vary from discipline to discipline but usually you will receive one very detailed report or between two and four shorter reports. We will discuss how to respond to the reviews shortly. For now let us spend a few moments considering what to do when things go wrong.

What to do when all goes quiet

As you will have gathered by now, getting your PhD published is a long haul. It requires careful preparation, hard work and a lot of patience. It is quite easy to understand the frustration you might feel after putting in all the effort required to write a proposal, you finally find someone prepared to send it out for review and then everything goes quiet, for one month, two months, maybe more. You begin to fear that your proposal has been forgotten or that the editor has changed their mind without telling you. Perhaps someone else will publish research which outdates your own or almost as bad, the book will never be published in time to help you secure tenure. Perhaps you fear all of the above. You decide to phone/write /email to find out what on earth has been going on and to try to force them to make a decision. You feel by now any decision is better than endless waiting. Don't. Don't let it reach the stage where so much time has gone by since you submitted the proposal that you have worked yourself up into a fever of anxiety (which may well come over as aggression) and the editor may well have forgotten about the proposal or become so frustrated with their inability to secure reviewers for it that they never want to see the wretched thing again. Instead try to prepare the ground for a (relatively) stress-free reviewing process at an earlier stage, when you first make contact with the editor. You could do this by:

1 Including the names and contact details of a number of more senior academics who are familiar with your work either at the end of your proposal or in your covering letter. Ideally they should be people who have published extensively themselves and are not based at your own institution.
2 If you haven't included any names in your proposal the editor may ask you directly for suggestions when they get in touch to let you know they are sending it out for review. They may say they want the names of potential reviewers or people they can talk to who know your work/know the area who could recommend suitable reviewers. Whichever it is, be prepared with the names of at least three–four people so the editor has some choice. If one of those people has published with that particular press, so much the better.
3 Alternatively, if the editor tells you your proposal will be going out for review but doesn't ask for any suggestions, ask them in your reply if some names would be helpful. They will soon let you know if they would and if not you have lost nothing, and shown your understanding of the process.
4 Ask what the likely timeframe for the review process is.

If the editor is reluctant to give you a timeframe within which to expect the reviews and you have not heard anything after a month or two I think it is acceptable to send a gentle chasing email enquiring how the review process is going and saying how excited/pleased you are that their press is considering your proposal. I have been careful to personalize this advice as many of my colleagues may disagree and I can already hear the gnashing of teeth and see the rolling of eyes that may greet this particular suggestion. Nobody likes to be chased or hassled; everybody has a bigger workload than they can manage. But precisely because of this it is impossible for all but the most dedicated and exceptionally organized to keep a track of every single project all of the time. The vast majority of editors do occasionally get distracted by more pressing or more lucrative projects and I personally do not mind the odd, gentle reminder with two important provisos: they must be politely worded and they should be merited. By which I mean if only a few weeks have passed since I agreed to send something out for review and it is the summer or there has been a major holiday or conference in the intervening time I would definitely feel that I was being hassled. If, on the other hand, a few months had passed, an email might well prove a useful reminder that I either needed to make a renewed effort to commission reviews or decide whether the effort involved was really worthwhile. For you should always remember that any action carries risks. If you don't remind a busy editor of your project it may well be pushed to the bottom of the pile or even worse slip through the cracks and be forgotten completely. But there is also the possibility that in the process of reminding the editor of your project you could just as easily spur them to turn you down as to find reviewers. It is a risk you have to assess and only you can decide whether it is worth taking based on your previous interactions with the editor and the urgency of your situation.

The one instance where (in my opinion) the benefits far outweigh any potential disadvantage and I would recommend making contact is when you have sent your proposal to a number of publishers and a couple have said they would like to send it out for review. If one gets back to you fairly quickly with a positive response (and chances are it's usually the one you are least keen on) then you must let the other publisher know and find out what stage in the review process they are at so you can make a realistic assessment of your options. It may be that a bird in the hand is worth two in the bush, but it might also be that an editor who senses competition works twice as fast! Obviously you will have to make a decision based on your own particular circumstances as to whether you should accept the first contract offered to you (and there are bound to be pros and cons) but once again the way in which you do it and the language you use are crucial. If you send a rather curt email along the lines of:

Dear Ms Caro

I was wondering if you had made any progress with reviewing my book The Cultural Politics of Adoption *as I have now been made an offer by another publisher.*

Yours
Janet Jones

You are likely to receive a response along the lines of:

Dear Dr Jones

Congratulations! I wish you every success with your publication.
Sarah

If on the other hand you write something along the lines of:

Dear Ms Caro

I hope you are well. You may remember that when you kindly agreed to send my book The Cultural Politics of Adoption *out for review I mentioned that I was submitting it to a number of different publishers. I have now had a positive response from one of the other publishers and before getting back to them wondered if you might be able to give me an update on the review process. Do you know yet when you are likely to receive the reviews you have commissioned and if so when you are likely to be a position to make a decision? If the choice were mine I would much prefer to publish with you for all the reasons outlined in my covering letter. I have therefore asked the other publisher to wait a few weeks but I obviously can't keep them waiting indefinitely so would much appreciate some indication of the likely timeframe for a decision.*

With best wishes and thanks for your time
Janet Jones

You are much more likely to get a positive response. As with everything else in this book there are of course no guarantees. The editor may feel with everything else on their plate that it is easier just to cut their losses and back out gracefully. With the added advantage that they need not feel guilty as you already have another offer in place. If, however, they were sufficiently interested in your proposal to agree to send it out for review in the first place, the news that one of their rivals has already made an offer may encourage them to chase up the reviewers and reach a decision sooner than they might normally have done. In such circumstances as long as the reviews are reasonably encouraging, you may well get a positive decision.

Receiving your reviews

Having briefly considered what you can do to manage the situation when the review process breaks down, let us assume all is going smoothly again and the reviews have come in. It is hard to believe that even the most seasoned academic author does not feel a slight twinge of excitement and a tight, nervous knot in their stomach when they receive the reviews of their latest work. Even so, if you have put a lot of effort into securing them and have spent many anxious moments wondering what they might contain, they can be something of an anticlimax when they finally arrive. Whatever your initial feelings might be however, hide them. Do not get back to your editor with a response until you have had time to calm down. Read the reviews through several times, discuss with friends and colleagues and then get back with a detailed and considered reply. This is perhaps obvious advice. It is also the kind of advice which is easy to give but difficult to follow as I know from experience being a naturally impetuous person who has had to work hard over the years to curb my tendency to speak first and think later. In the age of email, however, and almost instant communication, it is crucial that you don't reply by return email; possibly in the first flush of anger/frustration/ hurt at a critical review and by an intemperate remark destroy your chances of getting published completely. Go for a walk, complain to a friend, hit a ball, and don't hit 'reply'.

Depending on the nature of the reviews and how busy they or their assistant are at that moment, the editor may send you hard copies of the reviews or more likely they will send them by email. It is very rare, unless they are sending you more than one review and there are more reviews to come, that they will send without a covering note but the exact nature of the note may vary enormously. Generally, as a very rough rule of thumb, the shorter the note the less idea the editor has of what to do with your proposal; the longer it is the clearer their ideas. Like most things this can work both ways. If they send a long note detailing the negative comments made by the reviewers you will have to work hard to convince them that these points can be addressed or are unjustified. On the other hand if they spend sometime outlining the key points they feel need to be dealt with in your response, the chances are they are confident that with an adequate response and possibly revised proposal they may be able to get it approved by their commissioning body. Similarly if the note is brief it may be that the editor feels the reports are sufficiently positive to not need much comment or that they are so damning there is nothing left to say.

Whether the note is long or short, the reviews good or bad, you should acknowledge receipt within a few days with a brief email that indicates how soon you intend to get back to the editor with a formal response. If you are lucky enough to experience one of those rare instances where the reviewers are all positive, make no suggestions for change and urge immediate publication then you are of course free to thank the editor for the reviews, express your delight at their positive nature and ask what the next stage would be in order to move towards a formal contract. A more likely scenario is that you will need to send an email along these lines:

Dear Sarah

Many thanks for sending the reviews for my book. On a first reading they look as if they make some useful and interesting points. I plan to get back to you with a formal response by the end of the week but please let me know if that does not fit in with your timetable and I will endeavour to get something to you sooner.

With best wishes and thanks
Janet

The purpose of such an email is to convey the fact that you have received the emails, read them, appreciate the effort to get them, are aware that the editor is working to a timetable and that you are planning to spend time and effort on preparing a proper response.

Some general guidelines for responding to reviews

Having announced your intention to produce a considered and detailed response how do you go about doing so? Every review is different and it would be impossible for me to give you a formula or set of guidelines which would cover every eventuality. Instead I will draw your attention to a number of the most frequently occurring comments that are made by reviewers and suggest ways in which you might respond.

First of all, it is worth going back to basics. As discussed earlier, you should always give yourself time to think about a review and to get past your initial feelings to a more rational and objective response. Often a review which can seem overwhelmingly negative when you first read it doesn't seem so bad when you go back and analyze each individual point by turn. You may also find that something you initially thought was a negative comment may be ambiguous and open to interpretation and for that reason alone it is worthwhile sharing the reviews with someone whose opinions and judgment you trust. Don't just show them to a friend who will give you a supportive but partisan response. Such friends are to be cherished but at this stage you want someone who will be objective and confirm that the review is saying what you think it is saying. Or not. You should remember that writing reviews is not a scientific process. People sometimes write them without thinking fully about the implications of what they have said. They may be in a bad mood or in a hurry. Therefore responding to a review can sometimes require a certain amount of detective work to arrive at exactly what the reviewer is trying to say and what they think needs to be done to make the book ready for publication.

Having taken the time to understand as best you can exactly what the reviewer is saying, make sure that your response is written in as clear, as calm and as professional a tone as you can. Even if the reviewer attacks you, your professional standing or your abilities, don't stoop to their level. Such personalized attacks are fortunately rare and when they do occur they are seen for what they are and editors do not like them. They are interested in an objective assessment of the project and a vitriolic rant does not help them to arrive at a publishing decision. It says rather more about the ranter than the unfortunate object of their ire. Never attack or question the competence of an aggressive reviewer directly or comment on the tone of the review – unless of course it is terribly positive. By maintaining your own composure and being businesslike and reasonable yourself your response will inevitably contrast with and highlight the lack of professionalism in their review.

When you are writing the response you should bear in mind that not only the editor but also a number of other people within the publishing house who are not necessarily experts in your area are likely to read the reviews and your response if the book goes forward to a commissioning committee for approval. You therefore want to keep your response as concise and as clear as possible. You need to give yourself the opportunity to address the points raised by the reviewers adequately but having done so do not be tempted to then launch into a general defence of the project. The people reading it will not be interested in your own assessment of the value of your book but in how you handle the reviews. If you respond in a confident and professional manner you will do much more to impress them than by anything else you might say.

Try to open your response on a positive note. A good way to start is by thanking the editor for the reviews and the opportunity to respond to them. Even if you don't feel particularly grateful it shows an appreciation of the process and openness to feedback and a readiness to learn which are both essential and attractive in a prospective author and likely to enhance your chances of securing a contract.

Next go through the review or reviews picking out the positive points. Don't dwell on them too long but just enough to ensure that the reader is aware of them and has taken them on board. Once you have set a positive tone you can then address those points where the reviewer was either querying whether something was going to be covered (if yes, say briefly where and how, if no, explain why not) or asking about coverage of the existing literature (don't be afraid to say that you will not be covering something because it is not directly relevant to your argument). You may also have to answer queries along the lines of 'this is a very competent summary of the existing literature but it is not clear what original contribution it will make.' This can be particularly frustrating if you have spent quite a lot of time in your proposal addressing this very question. But don't despair or get angry, simply reiterate patiently and clearly what you think your original contribution is, whether it be theoretical, new research, a new topic, or a new take on an old topic or a combination of all of the above. It may be that the reviewer does not think it is as original as you do, in which case there is not much you can do but where you believe the reviewer has failed to properly understand what you are trying to do or has completely misunderstood it altogether, I think it is permissible to say so as long as you do it in as tactful a way as possible.

Reviewers often make suggestions for expanding either the overall scope of the book or for including specific extra material and you should address these next. Generally being open to new ideas is perceived as a good thing in a potential author so if you can take on board suggestions for including new material that will improve the book, do. Even if you have reservations about whether the material is strictly relevant you should indicate your willingness to consider it seriously. Expanding the overall scope of the book is slightly riskier. If the editor has already signalled to you that this is something they would like you to consider, fine. But if not you should bear in mind that broadening the coverage is likely to bring you into competition with more established authors and leave you vulnerable to criticism when the book is finally finished if you undertake to cover areas in which you are not really competent. There is absolutely nothing wrong with saying that at present you feel more comfortable keeping within the parameters you have already set, though if you wanted to you could propose some additional contextual or comparative material.

Finally you should deal with the overt criticisms. These could cover anything from missing literature references to clumsy structure and poor writing style, to a profound ideological disagreement. With the latter there is little you can do other than to point out that it is what it is, a theoretical or philosophical difference of view which should not affect the judgment of the scholarly merits of the project.

Less easy to respond to was another criticism I read in a report a colleague had commissioned of a recent thesis that claimed the author had misunderstood a particular theory that was key to the area and that this failure to fully comprehend the theory compromised the whole premise upon which the proposed book was based. This is a pretty damning comment but it is also a surprising one as one would have thought that if there was such a profound problem with the thesis it would have been picked up either by the author's supervisor or by the external examiners. If, however, you are faced with a comment like this you can try arguing your corner (perhaps having consulted with your supervisor) but your chances of a contract are probably pretty slim.

Missing literature references on the other hand can easily be included and where they are especially obscure, you can thank the reviewer for bringing them to your attention and promise to follow them up. The structure of a book is one of the most difficult things to get right. If you feel the criticisms the reviewer has made of the overall structure of the book or of the ordering of material within chapters are valid, not only express your willingness to take them on board but produce a revised table of contents incorporating them to show you are serious. If you don't feel they are valid, say so and explain why.

Accusations of a poor writing style are among the most difficult to refute and you may well find that you are damned if you do, damned if you don't. If you do you can sound as if you are protesting too much, but if you don't your silence may be taken as a tacit admission of weakness in that area. Generally I would say that whether you like someone's writing style is a matter of taste, but with academic writing taste shouldn't really come in to it. Good academic writing should be clear, direct, properly punctuated and avoid excessive use of jargon. If your proposal/draft manuscript does all of these things don't worry too much. If you find it difficult to judge your own writing and have not received any feedback from colleagues and friends who have read your work, ask them to be honest with you and tell you if they have any comments to make about your writing style. You yourself should have a reasonable idea after years of school and university whether you can write a good essay or not and if in the end you have to admit that writing isn't your strong point, you should seriously reconsider whether writing a book instead of journal articles really makes sense. If after further consideration you are still committed to a book you can either bring in a co-author who is good at writing or promise to have a colleague read it or even engage a professional to read it for style and do a language edit. This may be an especially attractive option if English is not your first language, not only for you but also for the publisher who may be reluctant to take on your book if they fear that the manuscript you submit may need heavy language editing which is not only time-consuming but also costly.

Finally, what do you do when you receive two completely contradictory reviews? This is not entirely unheard of and presents a real conundrum for both author and editor. If the editor was not terribly enthusiastic about the project in the first place, they may use it as an opportunity to reject the project. If they are genuinely uncertain or mildly supportive they will commission another review as a kind of tie-breaker. It is unlikely nowadays, with most editors bound by the rulings of commissioning committees, that you will have the same experience as Professor Robert J. Sternberg, a leading researcher on intelligence:

> When I wrote my first book, *Intelligence, Information Processing, and Analogical Reasoning* (1977) based on my thesis, I had contracted for it with Larry Erlbaum. I then received two reviews. One of them was neutral. The other was 17 pages, single-spaced, and almost entirely negative. Larry published it anyway and it later became a citation classic.

But I guess one can always hope and as discussed below, if things don't work out there are always other avenues to explore.

Coping with rejection

The most difficult aspect of the whole process of trying to get published is coping with rejection. None of us enjoy it, but some people seem to manage it better than others. I am sure that this partly depends on personality and other factors one has no control over, but it also comes with practice. If you have always done well at school, got in to your first choice university, succeeded at everything you tried your hand at, it may come as a bit of a rude shock to have your journal article or book proposal turned down. The key thing is not to take it personally. Much easier said than done, I know, but in many cases as we discussed earlier in relation to journal articles, an article or book may be turned down, not because it lacks any intrinsic merit, but because it simply doesn't fit the profile of that particular journal or publisher. After the first few rejections (and acceptances) you will get used to it. It is never pleasant but you will realize that it is a part of academic life and that even the most established academics have to cope with it when their article is turned down or research grant application fails. The important thing is not to give up but to try to learn from the experience. Having said that if you are sent a letter along the lines:

Dear Janet

Please find enclosed the reviews for your proposal. I am sorry to say that on the basis of these reviews we have decided not to pursue this project any further and wish you every success in finding an alternative publisher.

With best wishes
Sarah

– you have been well and truly turned down and there is nothing you can do about it. There is no point trying to get the editor to change their mind by arguing your case against the reviewers because the editor has already made their decision and moved onto the next thing. They will not be willing to enter into a debate and if you try to force one you will significantly reduce your chances of ever publishing with that editor or publishing house in the future. The best and only real option that is open to you is to accept rejection but not defeat, graciously. Just because this publisher has decided that your project is not for them it does not mean that another publisher will not be interested. With (at a conservative estimate) more than a 100 academic presses in the US and Europe that you could try, your chances of finding a publisher are pretty good. As discussed above, when an editor turns your book down they are not implicitly criticizing you as a person or saying your work is no good or that you will never be good enough to publish with them, simply that this particular project at this particular time is not right for them. All of which is self-evident of course, but strangely hard to remember at the time.

Finally, having come to terms with your rejection, what do you do next? Depending on what the reviewers actually said it may be that it is time to go back to the drawing board and rethink the whole project. Perhaps you need to reframe it, contextualize it within a broader literature or introduce a greater range of methodological techniques. Perhaps you need to consider again whether it works best in book form or as a series of journal articles. In short you may need to readdress the issues we discussed in Chapters 3 and 4 when you were first thinking about publishing your thesis.

Alternatively it may just be that you were unlucky with the reviews. On another day the reviewers might have been more positive and the editor may have decided it was worth taking a risk on your book. In which case do a quick literature search to make sure that you refer to any major new work that has been published in your area in the last couple of months, read any thing that may directly impact on your own work, revise the proposal if necessary and send it out again to the next batch of publishers. As someone, somewhere famously said 'It ain't over, til it's over.'

To sum up:

- Do include suggestions for potential reviewers in your proposal or covering letter.

- Do establish a rough timeframe for the reviewing process and contact your editor if you have not heard anything for several months.

- Do respond to the reviewers' comments as fully and as positively as you can.

- Do accept rejection graciously and use it as an opportunity to revisit your project, revising if necessary.

- Do send your proposal out to other publishers if you are still confident that it is as good as you can make it.

- Don't hassle your editor and constantly chase them for updates and reviews.

- Don't let things drift either. If you leave it six months before you follow up and the editor has in the meantime decided to abandon the proposal, you will have wasted valuable time you might have spent securing a contract elsewhere.

- Don't respond immediately to the reviews. Give yourself time to digest them and discuss them with friends and colleagues.

- Don't attack an overly aggressive or negative reviewer in your response. Instead let your own calm, competence contrast with their lack of professionalism.

- Don't take it personally and don't despair if your proposal is rejected as a result of the reviews, there is always another publisher.

7

NEGOTIATING A CONTRACT

Contracts can be very bewildering. This chapter looks at some of the issues you need to be aware of when negotiating your contract so that you can combine realistic expectations with an informed assessment of which things might be negotiable and which not. It takes a brief look at the issue of whether you should attempt to negotiate at all, and then the basic components of a contract including payments, subsidiary rights, permissions, index, copyright and delivery dates.

At a recent dinner party I mentioned that I was writing this book and currently working on the chapter about negotiating a contract. To which two literature professors who were there quipped almost in unison 'Well that should be a short chapter.' 'Why?' I asked. 'Because it will contain one word – Yes!' they replied.

I was a little shocked by their response. 'But do you mean there is so much pressure to publish in your area that any contract is worth having?' 'Yes', was the answer 'publishing your thesis is more or less a prerequisite for eventually securing tenure so if a half reputable publisher is prepared to publish it you should accept it gratefully and not look a gift horse in the mouth. Besides students can have such unrealistic expectations…'

As they continued it became clear that their views were not born from cynicism but experience, and given the very real pressures on young academics to publish these days, what they were saying was entirely sensible in relation to their own discipline. As we have discussed before, and will no doubt refer to again, the pressures to publish books as opposed to journal articles vary enormously from subject area to area. What is sensible advice for the doctoral student in English or American literature is not necessarily applicable to the social scientist. One truth, however, does remain, whatever your discipline: that if you are offered a contract to publish your thesis you are jolly lucky, but that doesn't prevent you from trying to secure the best, or at least a better deal, if you can.

The initial offer

So let us leap ahead now and assume in Panglossian mode that all is for the best in the best of all possible worlds. Your carefully crafted response has done its job and the reviewers' praises have been noted and their caveats put to one side. The commissioning committee has approved your book and that longed for letter or email has finally arrived with an official offer of a contract. Depending on the publisher the letter you are sent may include an outline of the key terms of the contract they propose to offer you or an actual draft contract for you to approve before the final version is sent to you. The letter will also draw your attention to any conditions that the Commissioning Committee has seen fit to attach to the offer of a contract. If an incomplete proposal was reviewed, the contract will invariably include the provision that the book will only be accepted for publication on condition that the final manuscript is read and approved by a reviewer to be chosen by the publisher. The reviewer chosen is often, though not always, one of the original reviewers of the proposal, but it is unlikely that a specific reviewer will be mentioned in the contract. This is standard practice and is simply a sensible insurance policy for a publisher to take out with an untested author or project, so don't worry. It does not mean that the publisher is only half-committing to your book. Even well-established authors may have such conditions placed on their contracts if they have only submitted a proposal and some will ask the editor to arrange a final review of their completed manuscript where no such condition exists, as a useful extra service.

As I have advised at many other stages of this process the best strategy is a speedy response which buys you a little more time for careful consideration. So acknowledge the letter/email straight away expressing your delight at the offer and your gratitude to the editor for their support and hard work in getting the project accepted, then promise to get back to them within a few days (a week at most) when you have had time to go through the draft contract. If they haven't sent you a draft contract you can always ask to see one or ask for a little more time to consider the terms on the grounds that you are new to the whole business and would just like to talk it through with a more experienced friend or colleague before finally accepting. However you word your message though, do make sure it is clear that you do intend to accept their offer and that you are not planning to launch into protracted negotiations. Whether this is your intention or not, implying that you are considering it at this stage is likely to make the editor considerably less sympathetic to any negotiations/requests you might wish to make in due course.

Negotiating your contract: some hard truths

The first and most important thing you should bear in mind when considering the offer you have been made is that life is not fair. If you are one of those golden beings who have been doled out more than their fair share of good looks, brain power and athleticism, you may not have noticed this before, but as you look at your contract, especially if your subject matter is history, literature or social studies, you will begin to see life as the rest of us experience it. Life is not fair but you have to make the most of what you have been given. If your PhD is in one of the areas mentioned above you do in fact have a far greater chance of getting your thesis published as a book than if you are a scientist or an economist. History, literature and sociology are all book-based subjects. The people working in them read books when they are doing their research, use books to teach with and write books to communicate new ideas. As a result demand is high but also, as our literature professors indicated, supply is high and with such intense competition to get published, the price publishers are prepared to pay for your book is low compared to if you were writing a first book in cognitive neuroscience or physics (both subject areas in which it is much more difficult to persuade people to write books rather than journal articles).

There are a number of different forms the offer you receive from the publisher may take. All of them are designed to minimize the risk to the publisher and keep costs low while still enabling them to give you at least a token remuneration. It is important when considering your contract to remember that neither they nor you are likely to make much money from this transaction and that its value to both parties should not be measured in purely monetary terms. I know, I am a publisher and I would say that, but to be frank neither of us would be in this business if money making was our major preoccupation. If you look at the commercial risks and constraints involved in scholarly book publishing no sane person would do it but academic presses still survive because there remains an admittedly limited but nonetheless real demand for academic monographs, both from young scholars like yourself who need to publish to further their career and from academics who want to keep up with the latest research/theory. The way these presses survive and manage to publish books which may sell only 500 copies in their lifetime is either through subsidies from the parent university as is the case with many US university presses, or by subsidizing the books internally with other, more lucrative publishing. These include local interest books (also a favourite of the US university presses) or textbooks, professional and reference publishing as is often the case in the UK and Europe.

So you need to have realistic expectations about the kind of offer you are likely to receive and consider any money you earn from getting your first book published an added bonus but that does not mean you cannot negotiate or attempt to secure the best deal possible, given the context outlined above.

Payments

The initial offer may be for a low 3–5% royalty or a slightly higher royalty that kicks in after say 500 sales, or you may be offered no royalty at all. At least one of the top academic presses only pays a one-off fee of a few hundred pounds for revised theses but I suspect this practice will change as fewer theses are published and publishers themselves recognize that they either have to believe in a book and pay properly for it or it is not worth doing at all.

Let us assume you have been offered a royalty of 5% on a hardback only edition. Exactly what is it 5% of? You should be aware that almost all academic presses calculate the royalties they offer on the basis of net receipts (sometimes also known as 'sum-received') rather than the published price of a book. Net receipts are the amount of money the publisher receives once an agreed wholesalers' or bookseller's discount – usually between 25–40% – has been deducted from the publisher's price for the book. This means that your 5% royalty will not be 5% of £50 but 5% of £50 minus the discount so nearer 5% of £35. This is one element of the contract which is rarely negotiable.

You may, however, want to question the hardback only strategy and be attracted as many authors are by the possibility of a paperback edition. It is worth bearing in mind, however, that if your book is realistically only ever going to sell between 500–800 copies then 5% of 500 sales of a book priced at £50 is worth more than 5% of a book priced at £16.99 – though as already discussed, neither amount is going to make your fortune. It may also be that publishing in paperback is simply not an option. You should check that the same royalty applies across all territories. Many publishers will, as a matter of course, offer a lower rate on sales outside their home territories as they may be providing overseas branches with books at a large discount. If this is the case it is always worth asking to have a flat rate across all territories as it is unlikely to make a huge difference to the publisher with the relatively small volume of sales we are talking about here.

If you are very keen to see your book published in paperback but the publisher has not offered this as an option you can always try asking if they would include a clause agreeing to a paperback after a certain number of hardback sales, say 700 or 800 copies within the first two years. If you do achieve that many sales there is a reasonable chance that there would be a market for the paperback and though there are no guarantees, the risk for the publishers are significantly reduced.

I mentioned earlier that the publisher may offer you a deal by which you receive no royalty on the first 500 sales but after that threshold a higher rate of say 8% kicks in. This may on the face of it seem like a reasonable offer as 8% is a good baseline royalty but personally speaking I think this is the least attractive option of all as you have no guarantees that you will earn any royalties at all and could well write a book that sells a respectable 500 copies in hardback, and earns a few thousand pounds or dollars for the publisher and no reward for yourself.

Royalties are generally not paid on gratis copies or damaged or remaindered copies either but all of this will generally be covered in some detail if you look at your contract carefully as will the drawing up of royalty accounts and how frequently they will be paid. Increasingly the trend is for royalties to be calculated twice a year, once at the beginning/end of a publisher's financial year and once in the middle. This means that in the first year the first statement may show no earnings at all or only minimal earnings if your book published just before that statement was issued.

Perhaps the safest option is the offer of a one-off fee of several hundred dollars or pounds. If for example you are offered £500 and the publisher is proposing to charge £50 for your book (which is still relatively high for a humanities monograph, especially if it is not a long work) once you have taken into account average academic discounts you will need to sell at least 350 copies to match that amount in royalties.

The problem with the one-off fee is an emotional rather than a practical one. Unless you are a professional writer and used to being paid a fee for a piece of writing and then moving on to the next project it is difficult not to feel that it is somehow a cop-out, an admission of lack of faith in one's own book. It may not sell more than 350 copies. It may, heaven forbid, sell fewer but one always hopes that it will sell more and to seek a royalty on one's work signals the expectation that there will be sales to earn from in the future and that your book will not be a 25 copy wonder.

As I have repeated many times before you must do what suits you best and that will depend not only on how keen you are to be published by that particular publisher but also your own personal circumstances. If you happen to be desperately in need of some ready cash at the time a fee might be the answer but you might also try negotiating a small fee or advance of say £300 and a royalty that kicks in after 500 sales thus securing the best of both options. You might not succeed but it's always worth a try and you never know, you might catch the publisher on a day when they are feeling generous!

Subsidiary rights

As well as covering the basic payments for the hard copy sales of the book there will be a section of the contract devoted to subsidiary rights. Put simply, subsidiary rights clauses cover all the different ways of making money from your copyright other than simply publishing it as a book in English. The clauses likely to be of most relevance to you in this instance are those covering the percentage that will be paid to you of any monies the publisher generates by selling the foreign language rights of your book to other publishers, reproduction fees (if for example another publisher wants to reproduce a chapter of your book in a reader or edited collection), and increasingly electronic rights. The first two, foreign rights and reproduction fees tend to be around an industry norm of 40%. With electronic rights most traditional publishers tend to offer a fairly small percentage (around 5%) but it may be worth your while asking if there is any flexibility on this as industry standards are slowly changing. This is in part due to pressure from authors and in part due to the fact that the amounts of revenue that can be generated from electronic rights are becoming increasingly significant as the ways in which these rights can be exploited multiply exponentially with the development of new electronic publishing models.

Permissions

There tends to be, however, little variation in permission clauses which place the onus on the author to clear and secure any textual or illustrative permissions necessary for their book. This means that if you wish to quote extensively from another work or to use photographs, tables, figures or graphs that are under copyright it is your responsibility to find out who holds that copyright and approach them to request permission and pay any fees that they demand in return. If you are slightly intimidated by the prospect of having to secure your own permissions the publisher will almost certainly be able to provide you with sample permissions request letters and detailed guidance as to how to go about it but it does make it worth keeping all such material down to a minimum. Apart from very rare circumstances (such as quoting your favourite pop song lyrics) you should not need to seek permission to reproduce text under Fair-Dealing which is an international agreement by which the author of a scholarly text can quote up to a maximum of 400 consecutive words from another text as long as it is referenced clearly and discussion of the quote is integral to the argument of the book. Illustrative permissions are trickier. It is perfectly acceptable to adapt figures, graphs and tables from another work as long as you indicate in the caption that the graph/figure/table is 'adapted from/after Brown and Thompson 1988' but the end result does need to be significantly different for you to be able to use this strategy and you should always check with your publisher that they are happy with what you have done. Photographic permissions and works of art are much trickier and you will need to think very carefully about whether they are strictly necessary. If your subject is history or cultural studies or anthropology it may be hard or even impossible to avoid the use of such images completely in which case you might need to look into the possibility of raising some funding or sponsorship to pay for their inclusion (bearing in mind they bring with them a reproduction cost as well as a permissions cost) or asking if the publisher would consider paying for them up to a maximum amount of £200–300. Another option might be to ask the publisher to pay for them up to a certain amount but set the costs against your royalties so you are in effect paying for them but not having the stress of actually raising the cash yourself.

One further issue you need to consider with regard to permissions is if you are planning to rework material which has already been published in a journal article and use it in your book. You should flag this to your publisher and it will be your responsibility to secure the permission and exact wording of the acknowledgement from the journal publisher.

Copyright

The issue of copyright is a vexed and complex one that I don't pretend after however many years in publishing to fully understand. Although who will own the copyright of a proposed book is clearly stated in all contracts, there has in the past been a fair amount of flexibility with the way this has worked in practice. Thus even if the publisher had secured copyright in the text the author would be able to reuse parts of the text in different contexts – in journal articles, in other books, on websites – as long as s/he discussed it first with their publisher and properly acknowledged where the work was first published. My sense is that this flexibility is gradually being lost, which I think is a great shame and in the end benefits no one. Many publishers are becoming more rigid in their management of copyright restrictions as ownership of content becomes more important than the form in which the material is originally published. Conversely and perhaps in response to this, many authors are becoming much more particular about the wording they will agree to, even in contributor contracts for edited books and refusing to grant copyright and only agreeing to a one-off publication of their work accompanied by a whole array of stipulations.

With regard to your own contract there will be one of two options. Either it will have a clause effectively handing over copyright to the publisher or there will be an exclusive right to publish clause giving the publisher a license to publish but allowing you the author to retain copyright. These clauses are generally part of the standard terms and conditions in a particular publishing company's contracts and are not usually open to negotiation. You can always try if you feel strongly about it but if you are keen to be published you should realistically also be prepared to be flexible.

Index

One element of the contract which does seem to vary quite considerably from publisher to publisher relates to the provision of an index. All academic presses worth their salt will insist that your book includes an index but the majority are unwilling to pay for it, with one or two notable exceptions. I suspect this is due to a number of factors. Traditionally many academics felt that producing a good index was integral to the work as a whole and insisted on producing it themselves. This was partly because they didn't trust anyone else to do a good job of it in the days – not so very long ago but now almost impossible to imagine – when people didn't have search engines and relied on paper catalogues and indexes to find things.

Indexes from professional indexers have also become much more expensive to commission relative to the rest of the production process during the last 15 years or so. Most publishers have achieved dramatic cuts in production costs during that time through increased efficiency and outsourcing typesetting and printing to places like India so the £400–800 that the an index now costs is a significant additional burden and may tip a book over the edge from being just about viable to potentially incurring a loss. It is therefore unlikely that you will be able to persuade your publisher to commission and pay for the index on your behalf. Instead you will be offered a choice between doing the index yourself or the publisher commissioning the index on your behalf and setting the costs against royalties. Sometimes you will not even be offered this choice and the publisher will have a standard clause stating that they will commission the index and you will pay. Unless you are completely certain that this is what you want I would advice you to push hard to have the two options included in your contract. It is not difficult to include a clause to the effect that you will provide the index or the publisher will provide it and set against royalties. It won't cost the publisher anything and as it cannot be done before first proofs stage anyway, it buys you time and potentially saves you a large proportion of your royalties. With the aid of various software programmes and guides to indexing you may well find that it is not as intimidating a task as it first seems, especially if you think about the index as you are writing and/or revising, making notes of key words, phrases and names as you go along. If you are really certain that you haven't got the time, patience or skill to put together your own index you should take advantage of the opportunity to have the index commissioned for you but be prepared for the fact that you will still need to check it and may well end up wishing you had done the whole thing anyway!

Delivery date

The delivery date on the contract should not come as a surprise and should be the result of detailed discussion and consultation with your editor taking into account when they would ideally like you to deliver and when you realistically think you can deliver. You should make sure that you have a very clear understanding of what penalties there are – if any – for late delivery and if between putting together your first proposal and receiving the offer of a contract there has been a change in your circumstances let your editor know and negotiate a later date. It is never in an editor's interest to have an unrealistic date on a contract as these projected delivery dates form the basis of budgets and production schedules which need to be as accurate as possible. If one of the conditions upon which you were offered a contract was that the whole manuscript be subject to a clearance review before finally being approved for publication you should also clarify whether the delivery date on your contract refers to the final manuscript or the draft manuscript ready for review. Once you have established which it is (or even included both dates) you should take it as a real deadline and stick to it as closely as you can because if you delay too long you risk not only being beaten to market and losing potential sales but also having your contract cancelled and then all your efforts will have been in vain.

General disclaimer

One final point. The above does not in anyway constitute a comprehensive guide to book contracts and merely addresses the key points that are likely to affect you and that you may wish to negotiate on. Contracts vary enormously and the more authors involved and the more complex the project, the more complex the contract. If there is anything in the offer you are made or the contract you are sent that you do not understand or are unhappy about do not hesitate to ask the publisher to explain it in simple terms or talk to a more experienced colleague. It is important to remember with most book contracts that the people filling in the templates are generally not legal experts themselves and may make mistakes or omit to make amendments which have been agreed by somebody else. So as with much else, if in doubt ask.

To sum up:

- Do congratulate yourself on being offered a contract.
- Do ask to see a draft contract and read it in full before you commit.
- Do talk to friends and/or a senior colleague to gauge what the standard terms for revised theses are in your field.
- Do be realistic in your negotiations. You are not going to get a £5,000 advance for your first book or a 15% royalty and you will not be looked upon kindly if you ask for them.
- Do think carefully before trying to negotiate terms and be clear beforehand about whether you really want to publish with this publisher. If the answer is yes, be prepared to back down.
- Don't feel just because you have been offered a longed for contract that you can't try to negotiate on some terms.
- Don't hesitate to ask the publisher if there is anything in your offer of terms or contract that you are unhappy about or do not understand.
- Don't sign up for anything that you are not certain you can deliver.
- Don't throw away the chance of getting published for the sake of 1%.

8

MARKETING YOURSELF AND YOUR BOOK

Getting a contract and even delivering your manuscript on time are not where the hard work ends, you also need to prepare the (academic) world for your book. This final chapter focuses on some of the things you can do to maximize its chances of success such as forging a good working relationship with your publisher's marketing department, looking for opportunities to promote the book through conference presentations, workshops and seminars and letting your friends and colleagues know about it.

After many months of hard work you have finally secured a contract. Your PhD is going to be published and though you will doubtless have some revisions to make as a result of the reviewers' comments, the hard slog is over. That's the good news and you should feel a real sense of achievement at having come so far through a difficult and unpredictable process. The bad news is you cannot afford to relax yet.

It is a significant achievement to have your first book published but if you are planning a career in academia (which surely would be the only reason for putting yourself through this) and would like to have the opportunity to publish more books in the future, you need to do all in your power to make this book a success. To be a success it needs to sell. If your book sells it will help you develop a good reputation within your discipline and will lay the foundations for a strong publishing track record. It is, however, important to be realistic. There is nothing you can do to ensure your book is a bestseller – if there was all publishers would be millionaires and I would be writing a different book (*How to Publish A Bestseller*). You can, however, do some simple things to make your potential audience aware of you, your work and the book. And of course the more people who know about it, the more potential sales there will be. No one ever bought a book they didn't know existed. It's an obvious point to make but none the less true. Marketing, effective, targeted marketing is essential to the success of your book and without it your book doesn't stand a chance in a world in which even publishers would admit far too many books are being published and the number is continuing to rise year on year.

What to expect from the marketing department

Let us begin by considering what the minimum is you can reasonably expect your publisher to do in order to promote your book.

All academic publishers have a dedicated marketing department, though these vary considerably in size from publisher to publisher and in the way they are organized. The majority will be divided into groups along subject lines but they may also be sub-divided according to types of books reflecting the range of product of that particular publisher. So you may find yourself working with a marketing person who specializes in promoting academic and scholarly works across the humanities but you could just as easily find yourself working with someone who is used to marketing monographs, reference works, graduate-level textbooks and more general books in just one area such as political science or geography. Whatever the organization of your publisher's marketing department, you will have one person dedicated to promoting your book who will become your key contact for all matters relating to the promotion of the book. While they will be your sole marketing contact, yours will sadly not be the only book that they have to market and it is crucial if you are to maintain a good relationship with them that you remember this. Though they will do the very best they can given the financial and time constraints they operate under, these constraints are very considerable when you take into account the fact that they may have as many as 100 new titles a year to promote as well as an even more extensive backlist. For this reason anything you can do to help them promote your book more effectively will be invaluable but we will talk about that in more detail in a moment.

For now it is important that you get an accurate picture of the kind of marketing that is likely to be done on your book. Obviously there is some variation from publisher to publisher but most academic marketing can be divided into roughly five main areas of activity:

1 The production of detailed listings in catalogues, on websites and in all other forms of publicity materials providing detailed and accurate information about the contents of the book, its length, any features such as figures, tables and illustrations, its likely price and publication date.

2 The compiling of review lists, i.e. lists of academic journals and individual contacts to whom copies of the book will be sent when the book is published in the hope of securing at the very least a mention of the book in the new books pages of relevant journals, newspapers and websites, if not a review.

3 Direct marketing through an email or postal campaign targeting the people most likely to be interested in the book, these people's names having come either from the publisher's own databases or from mailing lists which are bought in from specialist providers. A special, time limited discount will often be offered to those who respond to the mailing.

4 Advertisements in selected scholarly journals, and specialist papers such as *The Times Higher Educational Supplement* or *The Chronicle of Higher Education*.

5 Promotion at relevant conferences and exhibitions either through leaflets and other publicity material or by having the book itself on display.

As indicated above this is by no means a comprehensive list but it is indicative of the kinds of activity you can expect. You will also notice television adverts and national advertising campaigns are decidedly absent. This is not simply because they are prohibitively expensive but also because they are not the most effective way of targeting the very specialized academic book market. The idea of having an advertisement for your book in the *New York Review of Books* for example, is no doubt very appealing on a number of fronts but it probably doesn't make sense to blow the whole of the book's marketing budget on one advertisement when the money might be better spent on a variety of less expensive, more targeted activities that are more likely to produce results.

The marketing plan, therefore, that is put together for your book is likely to draw on elements of all five types of marketing listed above but first and foremost it will focus on what is deemed to be most effective for your book, in terms of time and cost, rather than what sounds good. As we shall discuss below the marketing plan for your book will draw heavily on the information contained in your author questionnaire but it will be based on some kind of template that the marketing department have developed for books in your subject area. It will list the catalogues that your book will be listed in, journals that review copies are to be sent to, any advertisements (individual or generic) that your book will be included in, conferences that your book will be displayed at and any mailings that are planned. It may include other information but that will vary from publisher to publisher and book to book. You should be sent a copy of the marketing plan for your book at least a month before the publication of the book for your comments and input. If you are not, you should in the nicest possible way, chase this up as given the sheer volume of new titles to be promoted every year, it is quite easy for marketing plans to slip between the cracks. In large publishing houses with marketing operations in the US and Europe it may be that there are two different marketing plans and you should ask to see both of them and establish contact with both the marketing people responsible for your book.

What you can do to help the marketing department do their job

Having discussed the bare bones of the marketing you can expect for your book let us take a moment to consider what you can do to help the marketing department do their job as effectively as possible. By far the most frequent complaint one hears from authors is about the marketing of their book. In fact though I have never worked in marketing myself I feel considerable sympathy for those who work in this crucial but much under appreciated area. If a book does badly it is invariably blamed on the lack, or poor quality, of the marketing. If it is a success few academic authors will attribute it to the excellence of the marketing campaign but rather to the brilliance of their own scholarly insight. Yet if one considers the range of marketing activities used to promote the average academic monograph, the degree of specialist knowledge required, plus the sheer volume of books to be promoted and the time intensive nature of these activities, it is actually rather remarkable that so many books that will probably only sell 500 copies in their lifetime, receive so much attention.

Granted this argument is unlikely to hold much sway if it is your book being considered. You will want everything possible to be done to promote it and you will probably believe that it's sales potential is only limited by the amount of marketing that is or is not done for your book. Given the fact that academic marketing is time intensive and financially constrained, however, it makes sense not to complain about the marketing department but to do everything you possibly can to help them do their job. And there are a surprisingly large number of things you can do, though once again, you will have to use a certain amount of tact and discretion in your dealings with your marketing person. It is important that in your enthusiasm to help you don't give the impression that you are trying to tell them how to do their job, or that you think they are incapable of doing their job properly. Nor do you want to appear to be making unreasonable demands. Not that all publishing professionals are exceptionally sensitive creatures, but nobody enjoys being patronized and the most productive relationships are based on collaboration and mutual respect.

The author questionnaire

The first and most important contribution you can make to the effective marketing of your book is to spend several hours thinking about and then filling in a form that you may well be sent with your contract although it may not be possible to fully complete it until the book itself is ready to hand over. This form will have a slightly different title from publisher to publisher but they are all variations along the theme of 'Author Questionnaire', 'Author Information Sheet', 'Author Publicity Form' or 'Marketing Questionnaire.' Whatever its exact nomenclature, this document will form the key stone of the marketing campaign that is put together for your book and the basis for your marketing plan so every bit of effort and time you put into filling it in will be amply repaid. As hinted at before, the marketing person working on your book will be a marketing professional but they will not necessarily be a subject specialist so any information you can provide that will help them to understand the content of your book more clearly and its principle audience and markets will be incredibly valuable. This is especially true of books with a significant scientific or technical component.

The most obvious section of the author questionnaire that this applies to is that in which you will be asked to write a short – say 300 words – summary of the book that could be used on the back cover or in publicity material. You may well be asked to write two versions, a technical description and one for a non-specialist audience. Many authors ignore this request, assuming that someone else will do it for them but in my experience this is a serious mistake. Who knows the book better than the author? For while the editor may have read some of it, the marketing person will certainly not have had a chance to read more than a few pages of the introduction, if they have seen the manuscript at all before they start marketing it, and will be reliant on secondary material such as the editor's original publishing proposal or the initial reviews. It is therefore well worth spending time on this even though it may take several drafts to arrive at a description that sets the book in context, outlines its scope and highlights the original contribution that it makes, as well as indicating likely readership and level, all within a very tight word limit. Writing good blurbs is a real skill (and certainly one of the most difficult things I ever have to do) so don't be surprised if it does take several attempts to get it right and do be prepared for the fact that the blurb you supply may well be edited slightly to take account of a word limit or some additional point that you may not have mentioned. The important thing is that you will have provided the expert knowledge and insight around which the description can be crafted.

After the description of the book there will usually be a section asking you to list its key selling points. This should not take you long to fill in, but again it is worth the effort as the marketing person may be aware of the more obvious points but not all of them. In addition to those sections of the form designed to gather as much information as possible about the book itself, there will also be questions directly relating to the marketing campaign, asking you for example to list the journals that you think review copies should be sent to and the dates and details of conferences where the book might be promoted. Although the marketing person may be able to put some of this information together themselves and will cross check your completed form with their databases, you should not take anything for granted or assume they know about particular journals or conferences. Include everything that you think is genuinely relevant from the more general journals and conferences covering the whole discipline to the more specialist journals and events focusing on the specific area covered by your book. Marketing departments are usually very conscientious about sending out review copies so this is a good way to make people in your discipline aware of your book and even if it is not possible to have your book on display at every single conference an effort will be made to send books or publicity materials to as many as is practicable.

Increasingly publishers are aware of the opportunities to promote books online but it can be difficult for them to find details of more specialist websites and discussion groups (mainly because of the time involved in tracking them down) which makes this another area on which you can usefully provide information or guidance to the marketing department based on your own first-hand knowledge of the field.

Lastly, most of these documents will conclude with a section where you can include details of individuals to whom you feel a gratis copy of the book could usefully be sent for promotional purposes. These copies will be sent at the discretion of the publisher and they may even ask you to explain why you have recommended each individual so my advice would be not to get carried away and list the top 100 people in the field or all your friends and relations but to restrict the list to a maximum of about 20 and if you have the space and time include a brief description of each e.g., 'leading opinion former', 'might provide an endorsement,' or 'might include book on recommended reading list for course.'

Once you have provided the marketing department with as much information as you can at this initial stage of the marketing campaign there are a number of ways you can complement their activities, though some will need more advance planning than others.

Previewing your material: journal articles, working papers and online dissemination

As was mentioned briefly at the end of Chapter 2 on deciding whether to go for books or articles, it is possible to have the best of both worlds by doing both. You can publish a book and a journal article drawing on the same source material (your thesis) as long as you ensure that they complement rather than detract from each other. This should not be a problem as long as you remember from the discussion of different genres of academic writing in Chapter 3 that journal articles and scholarly monographs do have different formats and different audiences but they also have a number of similarities. These similarities (both assume a fair amount of prior knowledge, appeal to a specialist market, and have a clear argument and structure) mean that it is relatively easy to put together an article drawing on one aspect of your thesis that will not only stand up as an interesting article in its own right but will also act as a preview or taster for the whole monograph. You do not strictly speaking have to request your publisher's permission but you will have to decide and agree with the journal and the book publisher which publication will come first and make sure that each is properly referenced in the other format. Generally speaking the article will come first thus enabling you to include a note on the future publication of the book which will serve as a very effective advertisement but if the article comes within six months of publication it can also serve as a useful extra boost to the profile of your work and hopefully by extension, to your book sales.

Some authors, especially those working for large research institutions that have their own working papers or occasional papers series like to use this format to promote their work. Whatever you decide to do it is important that you talk it through with your publisher and alert them to the timing so that the marketing department can discuss with you and exploit any opportunities that might arise as a result of this additional dissemination.

Academics and publishers are familiar with the potential benefits and snares of this form of complementary publishing. What neither has quite come to grips with yet is the impact of open access where material is freely available online side by side with the same (or very similar) material in a format, either electronic or paper, that is not free. Most academic publishers are happy to make one or two sample chapters of a forth coming book available on their website before publication and many actively encourage their authors to do the same. They recognize that the material can act as a teaser or taster in much the same way as a journal article can. By placing for example the table of contents, introduction and one other chapter online they are enabling potential purchasers to see what the book will cover and get a sense of the style and level of the material. What they tend to not be very happy about is finding the whole unedited manuscript available to download either from the author's or some discussion group or society website. Authors who do this clearly believe that the publicity their work will attract in this way will help to fuel sales of their book when eventually published but I am not convinced. Quite apart from the fact that such authors may well be breaching the terms of their contract, it seems to me self evident that if something is available for free or at say £50 most people are going to go for the free option. There is the argument (touched upon in the first chapter) that having established that the material is of interest the greater user friendliness of the printed book over a print out will encourage people to purchase it. This is true up to a certain point but it doesn't take into account the fact that we have all purchased books because we are especially interested in one or two chapters rather than the whole book. If people can cherry pick the material that they want and leave the material they don't want, again why buy the book? Though there is no hard evidence that I am aware of yet, my instinct is that there must inevitably be a fairly close correlation between the amount of a book that is available for free online and its print or electronic sales.

Conferences

Another way to promote yourself and your book is to jump head first on to the merry-go-round that is the academic conference circuit. You may not have had much experience of academic conferences and the prospect of actively participating in one rather than simply attending may be rather intimidating (not to say terrifying) but if you can screw up your courage and find the necessary funding it will not only prove a good way to promote your work but also an invaluable way to build up your personal profile and the necessary contacts for a successful career in academia. As you will probably have realized already, academia is like any other sphere of human activity. Success depends as much on who you know (and who knows you) as it does on what you know. This is also true for your book: its success will be determined not only by what is in it (the assumption being that it would not have been published in the first place if it was not of a certain quality and originality) but also by who knows you and your work.

Submitting and, if you are accepted, presenting papers at the key conferences in your area will provide you with many excellent opportunities to publicize your work and your book. People are more likely to remember your name if they have seen you giving a paper and if you are sensible and give the paper the same title as your book or one very similar to it, it will act as a trigger when the book is published. They won't necessarily remember what your paper was about or who you are but they will remember that they know something about it and are much more likely to take a second look and even buy it, than if they have never heard the title or name before. You can also follow the example of many respected authors, and finish your presentation with a final slide showing the cover of the book and the basic bibliographic information – publisher, price, date of publication. Don't be embarrassed about promoting your book in this way. Many people do it and in a world where so many books are published, anything you can do to bring it to the attention of potential purchasers is worth trying (well almost anything!). You can also ask your publisher to provide you with leaflets to distribute at the end of the talk or leave at strategic points around the conference if they are not planning to attend the conference themselves. If they will be there and you have made sure they know you are attending, they should have leaflets and perhaps a showcard on their stand/booth.

Another alternative if this sounds a little intimidating is to submit a poster. You may or may not attract as much attention as if you gave a paper but it can provide a better opportunity to make contact with individuals and discuss details of your work and the book and if you use a similar title to the book for the poster and include information at the end about its publication it can be an effective way to promote it.

Seminars and workshops

Academic conferences vary enormously in the way they are organized. The big conventions attract several thousand delegates, cover a whole discipline or sub discipline and are often organized years in advance and have a fairly fixed format. There will be huge plenary meetings, invited lectures, numerous themed 'streams' and business meetings. The next level down in terms of size of conference, but usually up in terms of specialization, tends to attract hundreds rather than thousands of delegates. This kind of meeting can often be more flexible than the mega-conferences and if you are feeling really energetic or simply can't find a suitable home for your paper you might want to consider organizing a session or workshop yourself. Find out who is organizing the conference as soon as you hear about it and see if there is anyone in your own department who knows the organizers or is even involved in developing the scientific programme. Failing that talk to your old supervisor and run your idea for a seminar or workshop covering some of the themes of your research (and hence your book) past them and see how they respond. If they are positive, contact some of the people who you would like to involve in the workshop/seminar and see what they think of the idea. If the responses you get continue to be positive put together a brief proposal and submit it to the programme committee. But remember although the chief reason for doing this from your point of view is to create another forum in which you can promote your book and yourself, it will not be a terribly attractive proposition to anyone else if you present it in this way. You have to make it genuinely interesting to the other people involved in the workshop/seminar by ensuring that they too will get something out of taking part in it, either through being associated with other established or up-and-coming researchers in the field or by highlighting a new or not very well known area of research. Or simply by having the opportunity to promote their work in the same way you are hoping to do.

Of course there is no reason why such a workshop or seminar has to take place within the context of a conference. It is perfectly possible to organize them within your own institution. The advantage of a conference is that you may attract a slightly larger audience (simply because there are more people around with a general interest in your area) but the advantage of having it at your own institution is that it will probably be easier to organize and you will have more control over where and when it takes place. You could even try doing both.

Wherever and however you decide to organize such an event though, a word of warning. Do be very careful to make sure that everyone who contributes feels that they have been given a reasonable amount of time to speak, treated fairly and been properly thanked for their contribution. Without wishing to be too melodramatic about the potential harm caused to promising young careers by slights real or imagined, it is important to bear in mind that people don't like to feel used or unappreciated and it is always wise to treat others in the way you would like to be treated yourself. Make sure you have an experienced chair or convener who will keep time, restrain the over-enthusiastic and keep the peace and do personally thank all involved in contributing to or organizing your event before they leave.

The book launch

The same advice applies to an altogether rarer event, these days: the academic book launch. I don't think it would be an exaggeration to say that most of the major academic presses are very reluctant to include book launches in their marketing plans or will even state point blank that they don't do them. Of course they do organize launches for a handful of star authors a year – successful textbook writers who need to be appeased and kept on board for the next edition or the odd high flying academic author who has made the break into a more general audience. But in general publishers do not arrange book launches for highly specialized texts such as your own, and with good reason. I don't know if you have ever attended one of those book launches where there are piles of books, lines of unopened wine bottles and rows of empty chairs apart from the bored looking PR person, a bookseller wondering why on earth they agreed to keep the shop open so late and a man who has wandered in from the street and has no idea what is going on but is looking for somewhere to escape from the rain. If you have you will know how thoroughly dispiriting they are. Such events do little to enhance either author or publisher's reputation and certainly don't provide a good return in terms of number of books sold (usually <0) in relation to the money and time spent organizing it.

If, however, you are still keen to mark the publication of your book with some kind of event you can always arrange or offer to arrange a launch yourself. First of all you need to think about how you can maximize your potential audience. If you just want to celebrate publishing your book you could arrange a party in your college or department and your publisher is likely to be quite happy to supply you with a pile of books, a couple of showcards or posters and some leaflets that people take away with them or use on the spot to buy the book at a discounted rate of say 20% off the published price.

If you would like to reach a more targeted audience you could ask your publisher if it might be possible to arrange some kind of event to make publication of the book on the booth/stand at a major conference. You have to be careful with these events as the sight of author plus friend plus publisher struggling to look as if they are having a good time drinking cheap wine while everyone else is ignoring them is not one you want to replicate. But if your publisher is willing to put a minimum amount of effort in you could arrange to have an event timed to coincide with one of the breaks preferably the morning or afternoon tea and coffee break (lunchtime is too long, too busy and people spend less time in the exhibition hall then) and instead of wine offer cakes or ice cream or cheese and fruit. Basically anything you can eat and that is free will be an attraction as most conference food is not cheap or great.

Alternatively you could try to organize an event in conjunction with your campus or local bookshop. This is the most ambitious option as a young and unknown author and not necessarily the best way to sell books but it will raise your profile within your local community. If you know a friendly bookseller willing to consider the idea of a themed event, you might be able to link up with a couple of other people in your institution, in the same discipline or a related one, who have recently published books and have a joint event. Probably a more enjoyable and less stressful experience and somewhat better attended than a solo event where all the pressure and focus is on you.

And finally, if you are too shy, too lazy, too busy or too disorganized to do any of the other things suggested in this chapter there is one thing that there is no excuse for not doing: include the details of your new book on your email signature and everyone you email will know about the book and be reminded of it every time you email them.

To sum up:

- Do be realistic in your expectations of what the marketing department can do for your book.

- Do provide ALL the information requested by your publisher in the form and timeframe asked for.

- Do try to establish a good working relationship with your marketing contact.

- Do feel free to make constructive and practical suggestions for further marketing activities.

- Do be prepared to put in some hard work yourself to make things happen.

- Don't complain about the marketing plan, contribute to it.

- Don't forget to tell your publisher about anything else you are doing (like publishing an article, posting material online) that might impact on the marketing of your book.

- Don't assume that your marketing contact knows about every relevant conference or opportunity to promote the book: if you hear about something new pass the information on in good time.

- Don't forget that if an event such as a seminar or a book launch is to be successful it has to benefit all those involved.

- Don't forget to have fun.

FURTHER READING

If you do a search on Amazon or in your library for books on academic publishing you will generally find two kinds of book, the general book on the current state of publishing and more specific books on how to get published (like this one). As you may have gathered from my introductory chapter, I am fairly sceptical about general pronouncements on the state of publishing but two books I have come across recently offer quite interesting and very different perspectives on the publishing business. The first is John Thompson's *Books in the Digital Age: The Transformation of Academic and Higher Education Publishing in Britain and the United States* published by Polity Press in 2005. Although Thompson, a Professor of Sociology at Cambridge University carried out extensive qualitative (and quantative) research, interviewing large numbers of people in the publishing industry, the theoretical analysis he applies to his findings derives from Bourdieu's concepts of social fields and capital forms so this is very much an 'academic' take on academic publishing. By contrast, *The Future of the Book in the Digital Age* edited by Bill Cope and Angus Phillips and published by Chandos Publishing in 2006 is mostly written by industry professionals or professors of publishing or library studies and presents a range of interesting topics and approaches but no overarching theoretical perspective.

There are a much greater number of the 'how-to' books readily available and most of them offer valuable practical insights and advice into the whole academic publishing process. For a comprehensive overview it would be hard to beat Beth Luey's *Handbook for Academic Authors*, 4th edition published by Cambridge University Press in 2002. A much-loved classic it provides a comprehensive and clear account of all aspects of publishing from manuscript to finished product. Another book which has garnered considerable praise is William Germano's

Getting it Published: a Guide for Scholars & Anyone Else Serious about Serious Books published by Chicago University Press in 2001. Germano is a bit like a favourite uncle, with a pipe in his mouth and a twinkle in his eye, guiding the would-be author (or indeed editor) through the publishing process and explaining how they and their book fit into the broader picture. A useful general guide to publishing focused on a particular area, in this case the social sciences, is *The Academic's Guide to Publishing* by Rob Kitchin and Duncan Fuller published by Sage in 2005. It takes a perhaps slightly less traditional approach and looks at all forms of writing and disseminating research including self publishing and publishing reports.

Moving on to books with a more specific focus on journals publishing there are a smaller number to choose from but one of the best is *A Guide to Publishing in Psychology Journals* by Robert Sternberg (who certainly knows a thing or two about publishing as well as psychology) published by Cambridge University Press in 2000. There is also *Successful Publishing in Scholarly Journals* by Bruce Thyer published by Sage in 1994 and *How to Get Research Published in Journals* by Abby Day, 2nd edition published by Gower Publishing in 2008.

This is by no means a comprehensive list but is intended to give you a flavour of what is available in printed form. Of course there are numerous websites and other sources of useful information, not least, as I have emphasized throughout this book, the experience and advice of your peers and your more senior colleagues. Good luck!

INDEX